Praise for Mark David Gerson's Books, Videos & Coaching for Writers

The Voice of the Muse: Answering the Call to Write
Birthing Your Book...Even If You Don't Know What It's About
From Memory to Memoir: Writing the Stories of Your Life
Organic Screenwriting: Writing for Film, Naturally
The Heartful Art of Revision: An Intuitive Guide to Editing
*Writer's Block Unblocked! Seven Surefire Ways
to Free Up Your Writing and Creative Flow*
The Voice of the Muse Companion: Guided Meditations for Writers
Time to Write
Write with Ease
Free Your Characters, Free Your Story!
Journal from the Heart
Write to Heal

Mark David Gerson is the best friend a writer ever had!
LUKE YANKEE – PLAYWRIGHT, SCREENWRITER,
AUTHOR OF "JUST OUTSIDE THE SPOTLIGHT"

*One of the most lyrical, spiritual and beautiful books
about writing I've ever read.*
JULIE ISAAC – AUTHOR & WRITING COACH – LOS ANGELES, CA

*Mark David Gerson will make your book-writing dreams a reality.
I know. He did it for me!*
KAREN HELENE WALKER – AUTHOR OF "THE WISHING STEPS"

*A skilled magician, Mark David Gerson is able to draw reluctant
words out of even the most blocked writer.*
CHRISTOPHER KEMP – CHATHAM, NJ

*I owe so much to Mark David! He helped me believe in myself enough to
write the book that got two wrongful murder convictions overturned.*
ESTELLE BLACKBURN – AUTHOR OF "BROKEN LIVES"

The catalyst I needed to set me free from a nine-year writer's block.
LEILANI LEWIS – KAMUELA, HI

Coaching with Mark David Gerson: Best investment ever!
CHRISTINE FARRIS – DENVER, CO

Without Mark David's inspiration, example and encouragement, I might never have had the courage to publish my book.
NANCY POGUE LATURNER – AUTHOR OF "VOLUNTARY NOMADS"

A highly recommended guide from one of the most creative people around.
WILLIAM C. REICHARD – AUTHOR OF "EVERTIME"

Mark David is a master...one of the great teachers!
REV. MARY OMWAKE – MAUI, HI

MORE FROM MARK DAVID GERSON

SELF-HELP & PERSONAL GROWTH

The Way of the Fool: How to Stop Worrying About Life and Start Living It

The Way of the Imperfect Fool: How to Bust the Addiction to Perfection That's Stifling Your Success

The Way of the Abundant Fool: How to Bust Free of "Not Enough" and Break Free into Prosperity

The Way of the Creative Fool: How to Bust Through Your Blocks and Unleash Your Full Creative Potential (coming soon)

The Book of Messages: Writings Inspired by Melchizedek

MEMOIR

Acts of Surrender: A Writer's Memoir

Dialogues with the Divine: Encounters with My Wisest Self

Pilgrimage: A Fool's Journey

FICTION

The MoonQuest, The StarQuest, The SunQuest

The Bard of Bryn Doon

The Lost Horse of Bryn Doon (coming soon!)

The Sorcerer of Bryn Doon (coming soon!)

Sara's Year

After Sara's Year

The Emmeline Papers

The Heartful Art of Revision

An Intuitive Guide to Editing

Mark David Gerson

The Heartful Art of Revision: An Intuitive Guide to Editing

Copyright © 2020 Mark David Gerson
All rights reserved

No part of this book may be reproduced, stored in a retrieval system or transmitted by any means, electronic, mechanical, photocopying, recording or otherwise, without written permission from the author, except for the inclusion of brief quotations in critical reviews and certain other noncommercial uses permitted by copyright law.

And no part of this book may be used or reproduced in any manner for the purpose of training artificial intelligence technologies or systems.

Published by MDG Media International
www.mdgmediainternational.com

ISBN: 978-1-950189-26-7 (print)
ISBN: 978-1-950189-27-4 (ebook)

Cover Image / Author Photo: Kathleen Messmer
www.kathleenmessmer.com

The Mark David Gerson School of Writing
www.gersonwritingschool.com

More About Mark David Gerson
www.markdavidgerson.com

Easy reading is damn hard writing.
Maya Angelou

The distance is nothing, when one has a motive.
Jane Austen

To my mother, whose infectious love of reading launched the journey that made this book inevitable.

contents

Opening Words	11
1. Getting Started	17
How to Use This Book	19
About "Story"	19
Special Note for Screenwriters	20
Guided Meditations	21
2. Why Edit?	23
3. The Language of Revision	27
Language Matters	29
Re-Vision	31
4. Finding the Vision in Revision	33
What's Your Vision?	35
My Vision	37
The Muse Stream	39
If You Get Stuck	41
Your Vision: A Guided Meditation	45
Now What?	51
5. Getting Intuitive	53
Your Inner-Editor GPS	55
Eight Ways to Awaken Your Intuition	57
Listen to Your Heart: A Guided Meditation	59
A Journey of the Heart	63

6. 12½ Secrets to Whole-Brain Editing — 67

- The Only Rule That Matters — *71*
- "The Missing Piece" — *73*
- How Does It Feel? — *75*
- Taming Your Inner Critic — *77*
  - Taming Your Inner Critic: A Guided Meditation — *78*
- Embrace Imperfection — *81*
- No Word (or Draft) Is Ever Wasted — *83*
- Your Story Is Smarter Than You Are — *85*
  - Talk to Your Story: A Meditative Journey — *86*
  - Talk to Your Story: A Quick Meditation — *87*
- Making Music — *89*
- The Power of Osmosis — *91*
- Savor the Journey — *93*
- Don't Be Like Oscar Wilde — *95*
- Your Best Is Good Enough — *97*
- In Case You Forgot… — *99*
  - Quick Visioning Meditation — *99*

7. My Top Twenty Revision Tips — 103

1. Break Free of Your Crutches — *107*
2. Make Friends with a Thesaurus — *109*
3. Convert Your Clichès — *111*
4. Get Active (Unless It's Better to Stay Passive) — *113*
5. Do More Showing Than Telling — *115*
6. Don't Overexplain — *117*
7. Don't Under-Explain — *119*
8. Be Specific — *121*
9. Paint Pictures with Your Words — *123*
10. Let Your Language Sing — *125*
11. Clear up Ambiguities — *127*
12. Clean up Inconsistencies — *129*
13. Eliminate Redundancy — *131*

14. Free Your Favorites   *133*
15. Write the Right Word   *135*
16. Double-Check Your Facts and Figures   *137*
17. Curb Your Exclamations   *139*
18. Be Typographical   *141*
19. Proofread   *143*
20. Be True to Your Vision   *147*

8. Slim, Trim and Simple   *149*
Thirty-Three Words and Phrases That Weaken Your Writing   *151*
Twenty-Five Damn Good Replacements for "Very"   *157*
Nabokov's Favorite Word Is Mauve. What's Yours?   *159*
Keep It Simple…but Not Too Simple   *161*
Trim the Fat   *163*

9. Refining Your Dialogue   *165*
Is Your Dialogue Doing Its Job?   *167*
The Seven Elements of Authentic Dialogue   *169*
He Said, She Said   *173*
Dialogue and Punctuation   *175*
    Seven Keys to Proper Dialogue Punctuation   *175*
    Punctuation and Dialogue Tags   *177*

10. Openings and Closings   *179*
Seduce Your Readers   *181*
About Your Ending   *183*

11. The "Heartful Revision" Mindset   *185*
Celebrate!   *187*
Revisit Your Vision, Revisit Your Work   *189*
Let Judgment Go   *191*
The Spirit of Heartful Revision: A Guided Meditation   *193*

12. Working with Your Drafts   *197*
General Preparation   *199*
First Read-Through   *201*

Second Read-Through	*203*
Subsequent Read-Throughs	*205*
Your Ten-Step Revision Checklist	*207*
Almost-Final Read-Through	*213*
Step Into Your Reader's Shoes	*215*
Once More...with Feeling	*217*

13. The Screenwriter's Edit Suite — 219

Six Revision Tips for Screenwriters	*221*
Your Twelve-Step Revision Checklist	*225*

14. Next Steps — 227

Now What?	*229*
The Seven Be's of Empowered Feedback	*231*
Your Circle of Creative Support	*235*
Testing Your Work with Beta Readers	*237*
Yes, Hire an Editor	*239*
Criticism Is Inevitable	*243*

15. Finishing Up — 245

As Many as It Takes	*247*
"How Do I Know When I'm Finished?"	*249*

16. Final Thoughts — 251

Trust Your Vision, Trust Your Story	*253*
You Are a Writer: A Guided Meditation	*255*

Share Your Vision — 257

About the Author — 259

opening words

Revision is one of the exquisite pleasures of writing.
BERNARD MALAMUD

Good style, to me, is unseen style. It is style that is felt.
SIDNEY LUMET

It's mid-1994, and I have been working as a full-time writer and editor for eighteen years. I'm good at my job, and I have an active client list that ranges from book and magazine publishers to universities, government agencies and corporate communications departments. You have to be good to make it as a freelancer, which I have been doing successfully for more than a decade, most of it in the highly competitive Toronto market.

But I can't do it anymore. Not the editing part. I can no longer spend my days as a professional perfectionist. I can no longer live my work life largely from my left brain, not when I'm trying to live the rest of my life more holistically...not when I'm seeking ways to be more creative in my personal and writing pursuits.

By October 1994, I have wrapped up all my current jobs, let go all my editing clients and retreated a thousand miles away from the hyper-bustle of Canada's largest city to the stillness of rural Nova Scotia. There, I apply the free-flow writing technique I have not yet dubbed "the Muse Stream" to completing the first draft of my first novel. It is as I settle into the radical rewrite that is *The MoonQuest*'s second draft six months later that I experience the glimmerings of a new approach to editing, a radical approach that runs counter to all the ways I have practiced the craft...to everything I think I know about the craft.

Without realizing it, I have created what I will come to call "the Heartful Art of Revision."

Problem is, I'm not sure how to describe it, let alone teach it. It's as though I *know* what to do, instinctively, but lack any conceptual awareness of what it is I'm doing...any intellectual understanding of how I'm doing it or why.

It will take another decade before I am able to grasp it clearly enough to include those glimmerings in the initial edition of my first book for writers, *The Voice of the Muse: Answering the Call to Write*.

Another decade passes, and I'm editing again — for others as well as for myself; no longer from that narrow-focused, analytical place that built my earlier professional success, but from that heartful, whole-brain place I have been cultivating since that second draft of *The MoonQuest*.

A book on editing has been on my to-do list for much of that time. Yet although I now practice this technique with great success on both my work and my clients' and although I teach the occasional workshop on the subject, I still feel as though I am missing the key that will make it possible for me to guide others with the kind of depth that a full-length book demands.

Then COVID-19 strikes, forcing me to recreate all my classes for an online-only audience. As I put together my newly reimagined revision workshop, one of those lightbulbs you used to see above cartoon characters' heads when they had an epiphany flashes above mine. I have found my key; keys, rather, for there are two: vision and intuition.

As with so many of our *aha* moments, I'm stunned that I failed to recognize their significance before this moment. The cliché "hidden in plain sight" leaps to mind because both words are not only integral to all my work, they have been woven into this book's title from the moment, years ago, when I conceived it.

Of course, just as editing is about more than vision and intuition, so *The Heartful Art of Revision* is more than a right-brain guide to the process.

No effective guide to fine-tuning your writing projects could be strictly a visionary one, any more than it could be strictly an analytical one. At the same time, vision and intuition form the foundation upon which everything else in this book is layered. Because without vision, there is no global creative concept for the many and myriad editorial changes every project requires. And without intuition, we are editing mechanically, soullessly and without discernment, something a computer could easily manage more effectively.

In drawing on *all* your gifts and skills, from both sides of your brain, *The Heartful Art of Revision* introduces you to a dynamic, cutting-edge practice guaranteed to carry you on a journey from first to final draft unlike any you have ever read about or experienced. It will revolutionize not only the way you shape and polish your creations, but the way you view them...and the way you view yourself as their creator.

Most important of all, *The Heartful Art of Revision* will transform your script or manuscript into the masterpiece it deserves to be...that *you* deserve it to be. Whether you're a seasoned pro or just starting out, you'll never feel the same about editing again!

Mark David Gerson
September 2020

1. Getting Started

Learn to enjoy this tidying process.
WILLIAM ZINSSER

It doesn't matter which leg of your table you make first, so long as the table has four legs and will stand up solidly when you have finished it.
EZRA POUND

How to Use This Book

If you have read any of my other books for writers or experienced any of my writing workshops, what you encounter through these pages will be at least somewhat familiar.

That shouldn't surprise you. When it comes to writing and creativity, there is little about my philosophy that does not apply universally, regardless of form, genre or medium. And it applies no less to your journey beyond your first draft as it does to the process of freeing that initial draft onto the page. When you get to Section 6 ("12½ Secrets to Whole-Brain Editing"), for example, you are certain to recognize my first secret: "There are no rules."

Secret #3 will be familiar as well because it underlies everything I teach and write, and not only about creativity: "Trust your intuition."

If I'm claiming that there are no rules and insisting that you trust your intuition, it would be hypocritical for me to demand that you use this book in a specific way or that you read it in a particular order. Rather, I encourage you to find your own way. If you feel moved to start on page 1 and continue straight through to the end, do it. On the other hand, should some seemingly random skip-about feel more appropriate, trust that.

All I recommend is that you visit the sections on vision and intuition early in your explorations. That's where you will find the foundation for everything that follows. I also urge you drop in on Secret #1 to discover how "no rules" applies to the heartful art of revision.

About "Story"

When I use the word "story," as I do frequently throughout this book,

I am using it to encompass all you would relate through your writing, regardless of form, medium or genre. I do that for two reasons. First, everything you write *is* some form of story. Even a grocery list tells a story. Second, it's a convenient shorthand that saves me from having to always list every possible type of writing.

Special Note for Screenwriters

Although much of what I cover in *The Heartful Art of Revision* either applies equally to screenwriting or can be adapted to screenplay revision, I have given you a dedicated section, "The Screenwriter's Edit Suite" (Section 13), where I offer a few additional tips and a supplementary checklist for editing your film script.

Guided Meditations

The Heartful Art of Revision includes six full-length guided meditations and several shorter ones, all designed to help you tap more effectively into your vision and intuition and move from judgment into an open, heartful, discerning state of mind. You can use the meditations in several ways:

- Record them yourself for playback.
- Have a friend or colleague read them to you, then return the favor.
- Get yourself into a quiet space and place, program your music player for five to sixty minutes of contemplative music (depending on the length of the exercise) and read the meditation slowly and receptively, following its directions and suggestions.

If you prefer a more professionally guided approach, I have recorded versions of five of the meditations on *The Voice of the Muse Companion: Guided Meditations for Writers*. Here's how to access the recording:

- Stream it for free as a subscriber to Apple Music[1], YouTube Music or Amazon's Music Unlimited.
- Download the album from my website[2] or from Amazon[3], Apple Music[1] or CD Baby.

As well, the quick visioning meditation at the end of "12½ Secrets to Whole-Brain Editing" (Section 6) is included as part of my video workshop, *The Heartful Art of Revision: An Intuitive Guide to Editing*, available from my website's videos page[4].

---

[1] https://apple.co/2CWhGtV
[2] https://www.markdavidgerson.com/books/voiceofthemusemp3
[3] https://amzn.to/3onwA5y
[4] http://www.markdavidgerson.com/videos

2. Why Edit?

Only amateurs think their writing is perfect.
ERICA JONG

You write to communicate to the hearts and minds of others what's burning inside you, and we edit to let the fire show through the smoke.
ARTHUR PLOTNIK

No matter how good you think your first draft is, chances are it isn't ready for the world to see. It is definitely not ready for a hired editor or beta reader to see, let alone for an agent, publisher or producer to see. It isn't even ready for your spouse, writing partner or best friend to see.

Every first draft needs editing. Every second and third draft also need editing.

"When people see the nice books with the nice white pages and the nice black writing," Margaret Atwood has said, "what they don't see is the chaos and the complete frenzy and general shambles that the work comes out of." Revision is the necessary process that carries you from the total chaos of your early drafts to a publishable or submittable final draft that readers want to read…and keep reading.

Those readers, by the way, could be the ultimate consumers of your published book or story. They could also be acquisitions editors at a publishing house, literary agents or, if you have written a screenplay, script readers at a film production company or prospective producers, directors or actors.

It doesn't matter whether you're Alice Walker, Francis Ford Coppola or Jane or John Doe. If you want your work to have its best shot at success, you must edit it through multiple drafts and revisions. How many? As many as it takes to get your writing project as polished as you can make it. It could be five drafts…it could be fifty. Each project is unique and each comes with its own set of challenges, regardless of your experience and skill level. Some of my writing projects have gone through more than a dozen drafts. A few have needed only three or four.

In the end, you want your book, poem, article, essay, short story or script to be the best expression on the page of your vision for it. And you want to make it possible for readers, whoever those readers happen to be, to follow your plot or narrative without struggle and to make your concepts, arguments and/or stories as clear as you can for them. Revision is what gets you there.

Remember: Even if you manage to attract readers to a poorly edited story, their experience is sure to be so unpleasant that they are unlikely to come back for your next one. Instead, do your best to get it right the first time. You might not get a second chance.

So don't send your work into the world just yet. Turn the page and let me guide you through a singular revision process that is certain to give your final draft its best shot at critical acclaim and popular success.

3. The Language of Revision

> The difference between the almost right word
> and the right word is the difference between
> the lightning bug and the lightning.
> —Mark Twain

> A language is an exact reflection of the
> character and growth of its speakers.
> —César Chávez

Language Matters

If you follow other writers on social media, you will probably have come across memes like these:

- *Write without fear, edit without mercy.*
- *Write from your heart, edit as if you don't have one.*
- *Write from the heart, edit from the head.*

I say, "Write from the heart, edit from the heart."

Why? For a start, the "edit without mercy" approach is profoundly disrespectful. It not only disrespects our creations, it disrespects us as creators.

Think about the language we use when we talk about editing. It's brutal and violent; abusive, even.

- We *force* the work to our will.
- We *gag*, *restrain* and *rein in* our characters.
- We *kill* our darlings.
- We *hack away* at our script or manuscript.
- We *hammer* our story into shape.
- We *punch up* our dialogue.

This is language that treats our writing as a savage that must be tamed, as an enemy that must be conquered. It's language that dismisses every un-final draft as an inconvenience and each deleted word, sentence, paragraph or chapter as a waste of time and energy.

No word or draft is *ever* wasted, regardless of its fate. It doesn't matter whether ten words or ten thousand disappear along the editing journey. It doesn't matter whether it takes two drafts or twenty to achieve excellence. Each word, sentence, chapter and scene you write is another paving stone on the road to your final draft...a necessary paving stone. There could be no published work or produced script without it. There could be no next writing project without it.

Yet, instead of celebrating the words and drafts that carry us to completion, we disparage them, and ourselves

We are writers, you and I. We know how powerful language is...how transformational language is. That's why we write.

Language matters. It matters in our writing, it matters in how we talk about our writing and it matters in how we recount our journey with our writing.

Instead of editing without mercy, edit *with* mercy. Instead of editing as if you have no heart, edit from a heart as big and open as the one you write from.

How?

A good place to start is with your language. Pay attention to the words you use when describing your writing. Pay attention to the words you use when describing how you edit. Pay attention to the words you use when describing yourself. And when you notice yourself employing the harsh, aggressive language we're so accustomed to using, *gently* correct yourself.

Edit *yourself* with mercy and from the heart, and you will have taken a huge step toward editing your work just as compassionately.

Re-vision

One of the things you will notice as you move through *The Heartful Art of Revision* is that I prefer the word "revision" to the word "editing." Although from a dictionary perspective the terms are largely interchangeable, the word "editing" often conjures up an image of red pencils making things wrong...the conventional, nitpicky, left-brain part of the process. Effective editing includes that, of course. But it's more than that.

That's where "revision" comes in.

Merriam-Webster tells us that the word comes from the Latin *revisere*, meaning to look at again. With the "heartful art of revision," though, we are doing more than simply taking a second look at our story. We are revisiting our original *vision* for it. And we are applying all our heart, art and skill into aligning what's in our current draft with that vision.

Red-pencil editing supports that process. But it's your vision that drives it.

What do I mean by vision? That's what the next section is all about!

4. Finding the Vision in Revision

> Vision is the art of seeing things invisible.
> JONATHAN SWIFT

> It's not what you look at that matters, it's what you see.
> HENRY DAVID THOREAU

what's Your Vision?

Do you have an overarching goal or sense of purpose for the writing project you are setting out to edit? Why did you write this story? What kind of impact do you hope it will have on your ultimate readers or, in the case of a script, your ultimate viewers?

The answers to these questions lie in your vision for this piece of writing. They may also lie in your vision for yourself as a writer.

What do I mean by vision?

Your vision is the light force of your work, the life force of your work. It's the spirit that is its essence, the breath that keeps it alive. Your vision is your dream for your work, the expression of your intention. It's what guides it, drives it and propels it from conception to completion. It's what guides, drives and propels you through every stage of your creative journey with it.

The more deeply you stay connected to that vision, the more fully your published or produced project will remain true to that life force, that dream, that intention. And the truer you will be to the work that has called upon you to commit it to paper and breathe life into it.

If you don't yet have a conscious vision, crafting a vision statement will help bring your story's aim and intention into clearer focus. A vision statement is similar to a mission statement for a business, but it sets forth a vision for your creative enterprise, not your commercial one. It expresses your most deeply felt reasons for wanting to tell your story and puts your passion for that story into words.

Once you have a vision statement, invoking it before you settle into editing acts as a touchstone, keeping you aligned with your project's energy, theme and focus. It guides your hand much as a jeweler might work, delicately etching the rough stone of your early drafts into the gem that reflects the vision your heart has conceived and received, then lovingly shaping and polishing it until you achieve the look and texture that most resembles that vision.

The vision statements I have composed for my books and screenplays have served as part of my gear-change from the outer to the inner, from left-brain focus to whole-brain focus, and have ensured that all my changes and revisions hewed as closely as possible to the project's true essence...and to mine. Then, once the work is out in the world, my vision statements have helped keep me centered, whether the work attracts criticism or praise.

A vision statement can be as brief as a sentence or two or as long as a page or more. It can speak in broad terms about your role as a writer or in more specific terms about your project's purpose.

Nor are vision statements fixed for all time. If you craft a vision statement in the early stages of your project, you may feel called to refine it to match new insights as you mature through the writing of it.

What's *your* vision? Don't think about it. Feel it. And when you start to feel it, write it. It doesn't have to make sense to your conscious mind. Let it be what it is.

On the next pages you will find four examples of my vision statements plus "Your Vision," a guided meditation to help you connect with your vision for your story and create a vision statement of your own.

¶ *See the exercises that follow Secret #2 and Secret #12½ in "12½ Secrets to Whole-Brain Editing" (Section 6) for alternative ways to express your vision.*

My Vision

My "Voice of the Muse" Book for Writers

The Voice of the Muse: Answering the Call to Write is about freedom — freedom to grow, freedom to create, freedom to write. Through a dynamic blend of motivational essays, inspiring meditations and practical tools, tips and exercises, it nourishes, nurtures and reassures its readers, inspiring them to open their hearts, expand their minds and experience, with ease, a full, creative life.

My "Legend of Q'ntana" Fantasy Novels & Screenplays

The stories that make up *The Legend of Q'ntana* have always been bigger than me — from the moment the first one insisted itself onto the page all those years ago.

These stories are so woven into my life that it is as though they live deep within my cells. I am each of their characters, villain as much as hero, and live each of their joys, triumphs, disappointments, betrayals and disasters.

For decades, I have watched their themes play out in the world around me, just as I have experienced them play out in my own life…not always comfortably. Now, as I feel new *Q'ntana* stories urging themselves through me, I see that I am more than the storyteller. I am the story.

Mark David Gerson: The Writer I Am

Perhaps the sentences I write are the seams that hold me together. Perhaps that's the real reason I write. Perhaps, in the end, it's the only reason.

My "Acts of Surrender" Memoir

Acts of Surrender: A Writer's Memoir is an exploration for me and an inspiration for its readers.

It's designed to open readers to the possibilities of freedom in their own lives and to the gifts of surrender.

It's about a life not lived without fear but in spite of fear, a life lived in surrender to a higher imperative, a life lived as the Fool in the tarot lives: in faith, and trusting unconditionally that all is good, all is safe, all is provided for and all is one.

As I write, I free my stories to reveal their innate teachings through the telling of them.

My job is to keep interpretation to a minimum.

My job is to recount and relate, to reveal and recapitulate, to walk the earth naked once more, clothed only in the truths that have revealed themselves to me through the living of them.

I open my heart to this story, my story, more baldly and boldly told than through any fantasy parable, as powerful as such telling can be and is.

I open my heart and reveal my vulnerabilities and fears (and, yes, revel in them) so that others may feel free to reveal, revel in and move through theirs.

Acts of Surrender is about the consciousness of freedom through surrender, awakening and revealing itself in the hearts of all those it touches.

The Muse Stream

I have explained the "what" of vision statements and I have given you some examples. Now it's time to share the "how."

In my books and workshops focused on writing, I explain the technique I use to write my books and screenplays. It's the same one I use to write my vision statements. I call it "writing on the Muse Stream."

Because *The Heartful Art of Revision*'s focus is on editing not writing, I won't go into the Muse Stream in depth. But I will give you enough of the basics so you can use it for your vision statement and a few other of this book's exercises.

What is a "Muse Stream"? If you're familiar with terms like "free writing," "automatic writing," "stream of consciousness writing" or "morning pages," you already have a sense of what the Muse Stream is about: a wholesale, uncensored, right-brain outpouring onto the page.

While we use those other techniques primarily as personal-growth exercises or to prime the creative pump, the Muse Stream is more versatile. It's a practical tool you can use for any writing project, from journaling through to books, scripts, short stories, poems, essays…and vision statements. Whatever you're writing, it will carry you from your first sentence to your last — naturally, spontaneously and without struggle.

I call it the Muse Stream because it un-dams the free-flowing river of creative output we all aspire to in all our writing. When we surrender to it, the words — *our* words — tumble onto the page as swiftly and readily as the waters of a stream tumble down their channel.

The Muse Stream is the place where writer's block not only does not exist but cannot exist. It's the place where doubt and uncertainty cannot survive. It's your direct connection with your creative source, that font of creative energy, inspiration and revelation we all have within us. And it's your direct connection with the soul and spirit of your writing project.

One of the beauties of the Muse Stream, and one that makes it ideal for vision statements, is that it gets you out of your head and into your heart. It carries you beyond what you *think* you know, feel and believe and reveals to you what you didn't know you knew. Writing on the Muse Stream, you *discover* what you know, feel and believe. You dive deep beneath your surface reasons for writing a particular project — or for being a writer — and into the core of your passion. And it's that core passion you want to be aware of through every draft and revision, all the way to the final period of your final draft.

How does it work?

Simple: Write without stopping. Without stopping and without thinking.

Too often, we think too much when we write. We think and we worry.

We think about where the next word is going to come from. We worry whether the word we're writing is the "right" word.

We think about what our vision should be. We worry whether what we're writing makes sense.

We think about spelling, punctuation and grammar. We think about paragraph breaks and coffee breaks.

We worry about other things that need doing. More important things, at least to our minds. We think and think and think...and we never stop.

Let's return for a moment to our swiftly moving stream. The water rushes from source to outlet in a frothy whoosh of easy flow, nothing impeding its forward progress. Now, drop a couple of boulders in its path and watch them hinder that flow. Drop a few more, and you no longer have any flow at all.

Each of your thoughts while you're writing can be one of those boulders. The more worry or anxiety linked to that thought, the bigger the boulder...and the bigger the potential barrier.

Here's what's going on: For the most part, we think with the logical, controlling, analytical, critical side of our brain and we write with the creative, imaginative, free-flowing, analogical side of our brain. And for the most part, when we do the former, we stunt the latter. When we stop to edit or engage our "thinking" mind in any way, we also give voice to our inner critic, that nattering monkey mind determined to control a creative process that by its nature is uncontrollable.

So when it comes time to write your vision statement (or anything else), write the first thing that comes into your head, then keep going, without stopping for any reason.

- Keep going even if you have no clear idea what to write or where the writing will take you…especially if you have no clear idea where you're going.
- Keep going even if the writing takes you in unexpected or uncomfortable directions…especially if it takes you in unexpected or uncomfortable directions.
- Always go with first thoughts. Second thoughts are self-censoring thoughts. Second-guessing is also self-censorship.

Write without stopping and trust that the innate wisdom of your vision statement will reveal itself to you as you write.

- Don't stop to correct spelling, punctuation or grammar. There is a time for refining your vision statement. That time is not in the midst of your creative flow.
- Don't stop to grope for the word that's on the tip of your tongue or to search for synonyms. Leave a blank space or type *xxx* and keep going.
- Don't stop to analyze or try to make logical sense of your vision.
- Don't stop to worry about relevance, redundancy or consistency.
- Don't stop to judge or criticize. Chances are you *will* judge and criticize. Acknowledge the judgment and criticism but don't stop to give it voice. Keep writing through it.
- Don't stop to read over, alter or rewrite what you have already written. Keep moving forward. Always.

Writing on the Muse Stream prevents your head from getting in the way of your heart and stops your personality mind from blocking the free flow of your authentic, uncensored, wisest and most creative expression.

Trust that what comes to you is what calls out to be expressed. Allow it to be expressed. Surrender to it. Unconditionally.

If You Get Stuck

If you get stuck — it happens — consider one of these seven techniques for freeing up your Muse Stream. With the first three, it doesn't matter what you write. Writing *anything* will nearly always dissolve all stuckness and reestablish an easy stream of words.

1. Repeat

Repeat anything to keep your pen or fingers in motion. Repeat the last word or sentence you wrote. Repeat the first sentence of the previous paragraph. Repeat the first sentence of your current writing session. Write and repeat anything, even if it's "I don't know what to write," "Who cares about vision statements?" or "This is dumb." Or repeat something like "la-la-la-la-la-la" (see also #3, "Write Jabberwocky"). Keep repeating whatever you're repeating until the flow starts up again, and it will. Don't judge the repeated words or phrases. However unlikely it may seem in the moment, some may end up as part of your vision statement. Delete the others once you're finished.

2. Free-Associate

Like repetition, free association keeps you writing while tricking your mind into relinquishing control of the creative process. Start with the final word of the last sentence you felt able to write and let it trigger another word — whatever leaps to mind, however silly. Let that word trigger the next, the next and so on...until the flow returns. Again, delete what doesn't belong when you're finished.

3. Write Jabberwocky

"Jabberwocky" is the nonsense poem that Alice discovers in *Through the Looking Glass*. When English words refuse to come, let Lewis Carroll be your guide and invent your own, stringing them together into sentences and paragraphs of silliness. This playful act will numb your mind and trick your inner censor into dropping its guard. Soon, nonsense words will turn into familiar words and your Muse Stream will resume its flow.

4. Change Languages

If English isn't your native language and you find yourself struggling, return to your first language for a time. It will boost your confidence and get your Muse Stream going again. If English is your mother tongue but you have sufficient facility in another language, switch to that language for the same effect.

5. Breathe

If you're stuck in your writing, you are probably stuck in your breath. Has your breathing become shallow? Are you holding your breath? Are you hyperventilating? Pause for a moment and take a deep breath in. Hold it for a few counts, then let it go. All of it. Do it again. This time, write "I am breathing in" as you inhale and "I am breathing out" as you exhale. Continue "writing your breath" until you relax back into the flow. The key in this as in the previous suggestions is to keep writing without stopping. Any way you can do that will help restore the natural free-flow of your Muse Stream. (Focusing on your breath may also help you retrieve words and images from the deepest wells of your inner vision and unconscious mind.)

6. Write Longhand

If you're on your computer or mobile device, set electronics aside for a time and pick up paper and pen.

7. Doodle

Draw or doodle. Make random scribbles and squiggles. Do anything to keep ink flowing onto your page. Before long, squiggles will make way for words, words will form into sentences, you'll be back in the flow of your vision statement and you will forget you ever felt stuck.

¶ *Read more about The Muse Stream, including what to do if you get stuck, in these books — "The Voice of the Muse: Answering the Call to Write," "Birthing Your Book...Even If You Don't Know What It's About," "From Memory to Memoir: Writing the Stories of Your Life," "Organic Screenwriting: Writing for Film, Naturally" and "Writer's Block Unblocked: Seven Surefire Ways to Free Up Your Writing and Creative Flow."*

Your Vision

A Guided Meditation

Allow at least 45 minutes for this two-part meditation and for the writing experiences that flow from it.

My professional recording of a version of this meditation is available for download or streaming as part "The Voice of the Muse Companion: Guided Meditations for Writers." There, it's titled "Vision Quest." See "Guided Meditations" in Section 1 to find out how to access the recording, as well as for tips on how best to use this book's meditations.

Part 1: Imaging Your Work

Relax. Close your eyes. Let your hands fall to your lap if you're sitting, to your abdomen if you're lying down. Breathe...deeply...in and out...in and out...in and out.

If you are setting off on this journey any later than first thing in the morning, run back over your day on fast-forward, and every time you get to something that was harsh or jarring, be it a thought, word or action — yours or someone else's — breathe in deeply and blow it out. As fully and noisily as you dare. As many times as you need to. Just blow it out.

And any moment that was particularly wonderful, breathe it in deeply and reconnect with the energy of that.

Continue to breathe, deeply, and focus on your eyes.

If you wear glasses or contacts, imagine, for a moment, perfect vision without them. Imagine unassisted clarity without correction. Breathe into that.

See white light around your eyes and your third eye, that chakra or energy center that lies between your eyebrows and above the bridge of your nose. See that white light cleaning, clearing and cleansing any blurriness, fuzziness, distortion. Feel all veils being pulled away, one by one by one by one. And as each veil dissolves, your vision becomes clearer and clearer and clearer.

Now, without removing all your attention from your eyes, move some of your focus to your heart. Be aware of the veils that surround your heart, whatever form they take. Simply be aware of them. Don't judge them.

Now, taking a deep breath, let the outermost veil fall away. Feel it fall away and dissolve. And when you breathe in again, notice that your heart feels lighter and freer and clearer. And as you breathe in again, another veil falls away. And another. And another.

Feel how much lighter your heart feels, how much freer your heart feels. It's okay if it feels a bit scary. Feel what you feel. Know that you are safe.

Keep breathing and feel yourself grow lighter and freer, lighter and freer, as you move closer to the heart of the matter and closer to who you are as the writer you are. And what a wondrous place that is.

Once more, breathe in, and if another veil is present, breathe it away. And the next. And the next. And the next, until all that remains is a brilliant light, no longer veiled and dimmed, in your heart. Breathe into that and feel it.

Now, let the light from your eyes and the light from your heart connect in a ring of light that circulates energy from eyes to heart and around again. Clockwise or counterclockwise; it doesn't matter. Whichever way it happens is perfect for you. However the light moves for you, allow yourself to sense it, to feel it. Your vision and your heart as one.

Now, see a second ring of light, moving in the opposite direction from the first, this time connecting your heart to the hands resting on your lap or abdomen. Again, be aware of the circular motion of this circulating energy. Around and around. A constant and consistent river of radiance.

Connect the two rings and you now have a figure eight or infinity symbol within you, as this inner light arcs from eyes to heart…heart to hands…hands to heart…heart back to eyes. And again. And again. And again, creating an infinite, luminous flow with your heart as its center.

As the energy circulates through that figure eight, be aware of the light pulsing in the topmost tips of your fingers, the hands with which you create, the hands with which you craft and revise, the hands with which you polish, hone and shape, the hands that form part of the channel that brings your worlds into reality, into focus. Perhaps you feel the pulsing. Perhaps you don't. Whatever you feel physically, know that the energy is there, the light is there. The creative power is there — in your fingers, in your hands, in your eyes and in your heart, as the flow continues.

Sit with that flow for a few moments, feeling yourself immersed in its river of light and in the creative power moving through you.

Now, move your focus away from the infinity symbol and back to your eyes, your heart and your hands. Let a beam of light radiate out from your eyes, another beam of light from your heart and a third beam of light from your hands — all meeting at a point in front of you, in front of your heart. That point in front of you, connected to you by all that light, is your work as a writer...is the work you are setting out to edit, to revise.

It could also be your body of work or a single aspect of your work.

It doesn't matter. Whatever feels right in this moment, let that be whatever it is in this moment.

So your work stands separate from you but connected to you, in that space where all the beams of light meet right in front of you, in front of your heart. There is your writing.

I'm going to ask you some questions about your writing. I want you to allow the first answer that comes to mind to be *the* answer. And I want you to know that you will remember it long enough to put it on paper, if that is where it needs to go.

So, focusing the beams of light that travel from your heart, eyes and hands and onto that writing space in front of you...

If your writing were a color, what color would it be? Let the color come. Note it. Don't judge or analyze it. Be with it. Know that in this moment, that color represents your writing. Be with that color for a few breaths.

Now, your writing is a space, shape or image. What is that space, shape or image? Again, don't judge or analyze. Let it be what it is. See it if you can. Note it. Know that this, too, you will remember long enough to write down or draw, if appropriate.

Now, your writing is a sound. Music, perhaps. What kind of sound, what kind of music is it, for you, in this moment? Breathe into that sound. Be part of it and one with it. Let it surround you and enfold you, filling you with its melodies and harmonies, with its simplicity or complexity. That sound, however it is, whatever it is, is part of you. You will remember that, too, when and if it comes time to put it to paper...or to sing it, if that is how you choose to express it.

Now, use your sense of smell. What does that tell you about your writing, about who you are as a writer? Is it a sweet smell? A smell that reminds you of something? Again, simply be aware of it, and let it be.

One more sense: What would your writing taste like, if you could taste it? Perhaps it's a food or type of food. Maybe it's a chocolate sundae, rich and creamy. Maybe it's comfort food — mashed potatoes and gravy. Maybe it's fresh, baked bread. Maybe it's a juicy pineapple. Maybe it's sweet and flowing like honey. Maybe it's spicy. Tangy. Tart. Let it be what it is. Acknowledge it. Be with it.

Now, go deeper still and let one word emerge that captures the spirit and essence of your work. Let it be the first word that comes, whatever it is. Don't judge it, don't analyze it. Don't second-guess. If it makes no sense to your conscious mind, perhaps that's just as well. Let it be.

Now, staying in this meditative space you're in, pause the recording and jot some notes about what you experienced — the color, the smell, the taste, the shape, the word...particularly the word.

Or take the word that came to you and write on the Muse Stream from the phrase, "['Title of project' or 'My writing'] is [insert your word]..."

When you're done, set your pen down and, without reading what you have written, restart the recording, close your eyes and continue.

Part 2: Your Vision

Reconnect with that energy, that space. With that triangle, that pyramid of light. Again, feel the light connecting your eyes and heart and hands with your work, your work as the writer you are.

Now that you have experienced your writing from each of your senses, move your directed focus away from those senses.

Stand above them. Get an overview of all you experienced, all the different connections you felt with your writing through sensing your writing.

From that vantage point, look down at that space in front of you where you and your writing come together, and breathe into that space for a few breaths.

Feel the fullness of it and the vastness of it. The specifics of it too. Feel all of it. Be all of it. Know all of it for the first time, again.

Feel, too, your connection with that part of you that is the writer and the writing and the work. Feel it and breathe into it. Breathe deeply into it.

Now, answer these questions:

- What is it that, deep inside you, you want to convey through your work? First answer. No thinking about it. Let the answer come freely.
- What is it you want people to experience through your work? Again, go with whatever comes up first. Don't censor. Don't judge.
- What do you want people to experience of *you* through your work?
- What do you want people to experience of *themselves* through your work?

Open your eyes, again pause the recording and note your answers to some of those questions, to whichever questions were answered.

Remember not to judge or analyze. Simply record your experiences, the answers you have received.

Stay in that meditative space and, when you're finished, restart the recording.

Turn to a fresh sheet of paper. At the top of the page, write: "I, [your name], am a writer. Through ['title of project' or 'my writing'], I..."

From that opening, write on the Muse Stream, letting what follows be as long or as short as it needs to be.

When you're done, sit quietly in the energy of that for a few minutes before reading it aloud.

Now what?

You have a vision statement...or at least the beginnings of one. What do you do with it?

I will have suggestions for you in the chapters ahead. In general, though, make a practice of reading it — aloud, preferably — before you start working on your project...whether you're still in the writing stages or are already revising it. It will always keep you centered and aligned with your purpose.

5. Getting Intuitive

A hunch is creativity trying to tell you something.
FRANK CAPRA

Intuition is the supra-logic that cuts out all routine processes of thought and leaps straight from the problem to the answer.
ROBERT GRAVES

Your Inner-Editor GPS

Intuition is your inner compass, your sixth sense, that nonphysical source of intelligence that not only transcends taste, touch, sound, sight and smell but is often more powerful and telling than those five physical senses combined.

Intuition is the language of the unconscious, the voice of the heart, the symphony of the soul. It is an expression of your highest wisdom.

Intuition is also the voice of your vision and, if you're open to it, it can be the GPS on your editing journey.

Unlike the GPS in your car, however, intuition rarely speaks forcefully or directly. Instead, it whispers suggestively, so softly for the most part that we must train ourselves to listen for it and attune our minds to trust it. It can show up as an "inner knowing," in odd physical sensations or metaphorically in dreams, synchronicities or other signs and symbols.

Its subtlety makes it easy to miss and its obliqueness makes it easy to dismiss. And although many writers embrace it at least somewhat in the writing process, most jettison it the moment they don their editor's hat.

Yet your intuition is as powerful a tool in refining your work as it is in creating it. As poet and historical novelist Robert Graves noted in the quote that opens this section, our intuition "leaps straight from the problem to the answer."

What writers wouldn't want to employ that potent tool as they shape and polish their work? If we can use what Graves called a "supra-logic" to bypass "all routine processes of thought," why wouldn't we? If as Oscar-winning writer-director Frank Capra put it, "a hunch is creativity trying to tell you something," why wouldn't we listen? After all, what is a hunch if not our intuition at work?

The good news is that we are all innately intuitive and we all have access to what Dean Koontz describes as "seeing with the soul." That soul vision — look at it as the vast wisdom of your unconscious mind if you don't believe in souls — can act not only as our editorial GPS but as our life GPS, if we let it.

The bad news is that too many of us don't. Too many of us have been educated to belittle our intuition and socialized to ignore it...to deprecate its infinite potential.

Yet if we nourish, nurture and practice our intuitive awareness, we can act on that potential and experience its innumerable benefits — and not only in our editing.

However, editing is what we're here to talk about....intuitive editing, to be specific. Here's how it works: As you become more adept as a writer, and as you free yourself to be more in tune with your work and its vision, you will gain an intuitive knowingness of what works and what doesn't, without always being able to articulate why.

That sixth sense — that inner compass — will also direct you to the appropriate fix or improvement — again, often without explanation.

The "why" doesn't matter, except to the part of your brain that always insists on reasons. However, as long as you have the "what" and the "how," the "why" is rarely relevant.

I have worked as an editor for more than forty years, and more often than not, I can't tell you the precise grammatical, structural or "book-learning" reason why something doesn't work in my writing, or in a client's writing. But I trust my intuition, my inner knowingness, my Muse — both to point out the problem and to suggest the solution.

By the way, your intuition can also communicate physically. In other words, you will sometimes feel in your body when something works or doesn't. So start paying attention to those signs and signals...to all signs and signals. Because that's how your intuition speaks to you. And the more you listen, however you listen, the more you will hear.

One final point about intuition: In the moment, it often makes no sense to our logical minds. That's another reason why we're tempted to reject it. Don't.

Eight Ways to Awaken Your Intuition

The voice of your intuition is never silent. Its wisdom is available to you whether you are motionless in meditation or rocking to your favorite band. At the same time, it can take practice to hear that voice clearly through the busy babel of everyday life. What follows is a selection of activities that can create optimal conditions for clearing your mind and listening to your heart.

1. Meditation. Do you have a daily meditation practice? Those twenty minutes can help you access your intuition. If you need help, the meditation that follows in the next chapter, "Listen to Your Heart," will help open you to that subtle, suggestive voice, as will any of this book's meditation scripts. Revisit "Guided Meditations" in Section 1 to find out how to access recordings of these and other meditations.

2. Go for a Walk…Anywhere. A meditative stroll will help remove you from your day-to-day busyness, silence your thoughts and free you to listen. A park, nature trail, beach or other quiet spot is ideal, although the buzz of traffic on a busy city street can sometimes act as white noise.

3. Get Moving. Work out or go for a run or bike ride.

4. Stretch Yourself. Take up yoga, tai chi or some other centering discipline that is at the same time physical and meditative. If you would prefer not to join a studio, stay home and tune in to one of the many hundreds of instructional videos available on YouTube and elsewhere.

5. Get Wet. Soak in the tub or take a long shower.

6. Exercise Your Passion. When we immerse ourselves in our passion, we often enter into a Zen moment of presence and receptivity. What are your passions, apart from writing? Spend time with one of them.

7. *Journal on the Muse Stream.* Initiate your journaling with one of the questions at the end of this chapter, or pick any random word to kick off your Muse Stream exploration. (Revisit "The Muse Stream" in Section 4, if you need a refresher.)

8. *Watch, Look and Listen.* Pay attention to your dreams and your gut feelings. Notice what causes twinges, tingles or shivers. Be aware of goosebumps or what Hawaiians call "chicken skin." Be on the lookout for the "meaningful coincidence" of synchronicity.

Which other activity (or non-activity) helps you be more receptive? Each time we take a break from our normal doingness, whether in the silence of meditation or in a heart-pumping workout, we open ourselves to the call of our heart, the voice of our soul, the echo of our intuition.

Exploration

Ask yourself one or more of these questions and let your answers emerge on the Muse Stream, freely, honesty and without thinking.

- Where in my life am I censoring or blocking out my intuition?
- Where in my life am I allowing myself to be intuitive? In what areas of my life can I be more intuitive?
- When in my life have I given myself permission to listen to my intuition and follow its direction? What were the results? (If you feel as though you have never done that, explore why.)
- When in my life have I had an intuitive sensing but not paid attention to it? What were the consequences? How might things have played out differently had I followed it?
- Where in my life can I be more open to trusting my intuition?
- What can I do in general in my life to foster my intuition? To nurture and encourage my intuition? To trust my intuition? To act on my intuition? What one step can I take today? Right now?
- How can I be more intuitive as I write? As I edit?

Listen to Your Heart

A Guided Meditation

Allow at least 30 minutes for this meditation and for any journaling experiences that flow from it.

A version of my professional recording of this meditation, titled "Write from Your Heart," is available for download or streaming as part "The Voice of the Muse Companion: Guided Meditations for Writers." See "Guided Meditations" in Section 1 to find out how to access the recording, as well as for tips on how best to use this book's meditations.

Relax. Close your eyes. Focus on your breath. Breathe deeply. In and out. In and out. In and out. Continue to breathe, in and out, breathing in relaxation, breathing in freedom...allowing any stress, anxiety or tightness to relax into freedom on your breath.

Listen to the rhythm of your heart. Feel it beating. Feel it pumping life throughout your body. Down into your abdomen, groin, legs, feet and toes. Up into your neck and shoulders, your mouth, nose and ears, your eyes. Feel its power in your arms, hands and fingers.

Feel that life force circulate freely, spiraling throughout your body, creating patterns and shapes, colors and sounds. Listen to the rhythm of that life force that is centered in your heart. And in that rhythm, through that rhythm, listen for the voice of your intuitive self, the voice of your heart.

What does it mean to touch your heart? Is it physically possible? Can your fingers reach back in on themselves, travel up your arms, past your elbows and shoulders, then down your chest to touch that central mind that, were it truly in charge, would revolutionize your life?

For, yes, your heart *is* your central mind — a mind more powerful, life-fulfilling and life-affirming than your brain, as powerful and magical a piece of machinery as that is. But that's what it is: a piece of machinery. A wondrous, miraculous machine, but a machine nonetheless.

When we let machines do our living for us, the result is mechanical, soulless and spiritless. It is no different with our writing…or our editing.

We don't touch others at a deep level when we connect mind-to-mind, though that connection is a powerful and important one. We touch others at a deep level when we connect heart-to-heart.

So let your fingers reach back in on themselves. See them traveling through your arms…on the inside not the outside.

See them reaching past your wrists and up your forearms, past your elbows and up to your shoulders. Let them stop there for a moment, and from their place deep inside your muscles, bone and tissue, massage and caress the tension from in and around those shoulders.

Feel the release as your fingers press deeply into the soul of your shoulder, releasing all the stress, all the fear, all the tightness, all the anxiety, all the "shoulds."

Notice the word "should." See it write itself out in your mind's eye, and see that this word "should" forms seventy-five percent of the word "shoulder."

It's in our shoulders that we hold all our shoulds. And it's from our shoulders that our shoulds must be released.

Now is the time to massage those shoulds away. Now is the time to un-should-er and feel the lightness return to your shoulders, to your entire body.

Now is the time to let the burden drop from your shoulders. Now is the time to unshoulder all you have been bearing. All the responsibility. All the weight. All the burdens of this time and all time.

Feel your fingers massage them away…out of your shoulders and out of your neck. Let the shoulds dissolve: "I should do this with my life"; "I should live this way"; "I should be careful not to offend"; "I should be careful not to rock the boat"; "I should be what others expect of me"; "I should do what others expect me to do."

Let those shoulds and all shoulds melt under your touch. Let that sense of lightness and freedom you were born with return, if only for a moment.

Once you feel the return of some of your natural lightness, once you feel some of that un-should-ering, let your fingers continue down to your heart — both the organ at the left side of your chest and the chakra or energy center in the middle of your chest.

Let your fingers continue down, and as they do, let them clear away any cobwebs, let them unlock any doors, gates or walls, let them move in gently and caress that place of love with love. Let the energy of that love, of that aloha, of that place of heart-centeredness, fill your fingertips.

Let the memory of all the love you have experienced, all the loving experiences you have lived, let that memory fill your body so that when, in a few moments, you take it back into your everyday life, it remains infused with that energy, so that this connection with your heart lives on beyond this meditation and can always be reignited.

Continue to breathe, to breathe deeply, as you open your heart and clear away and free all that has been scarred, barricaded and bottled up.

Breathe in the clarity. Breathe in the focus. Breathe in the love, the self-love, the love of your heart, of your wisest self, of your intuitive self. Breathe in the aloha.

Continue to breathe, in and out, in and out, for a few more moments.

In and out.

In and out.

In and out.

Slowly.

Deeply.

Fully.

As you breathe, listen. Focus your attention on your heart. Focus all your attention on your heart. In this moment, let nothing exist but your heart.

Listen to it. Listen for its voice, for the voice of your soul as expressed through your heart...for the voice of your heart as expressed through your intuition. Listen to your heart. Still yourself and listen.

Your heart has a message for you. A word, a phrase...many words, many phrases. As you continue to focus and listen, you will hear it. Clearly.

Once you hear it, write what you hear, if you feel so called.

Continue to listen, paying close attention to all you hear or sense, setting it down in writing if that feels right.

If you hear or sense nothing at this time, don't judge yourself. Simply launch your writing using this phrase: "My heart speaks to me of..." or "My intuition tells me..."

In either case, write on the Muse Stream, remembering to keep your pen moving across the page, letting it be the medium through which your heart and intuition speak to you.

Write your heart words, the words that express your intuitive sensings, your intuitive awareness, until you sense completion.

Then hold the silence for a few moments longer, open to anything new your heart and intuition might reveal to you.

A Journey of the Heart

I had been living in Portland, Oregon for nineteen months when the bottom fell out of my financial life. It was ten days into May 2019, I couldn't pay my rent, and my landlord had started making noises about eviction. I knew I would have to leave, but I couldn't see how. I lacked the wherewithal for move-in money, especially in pricey Portland. On top of that, I was living in a mostly furnished condo. How would I come up with the funds either for another furnished place or to outfit an unfurnished one?

I fretted for days, all the while fielding increasingly agitated texts from my landlord. At night, the prospect of homelessness kept me awake. Once dawn broke, I prayed for a windfall: a few new coaching clients, maybe, or some other miracle that would spare me from certain disaster. As each day progressed and no miracle showed up, I meditated on what to do next. The answer, always the same, was "wait and trust."

One morning a few days past mid-month, knowing this to be the morning I would have to tell my landlord *something*, my meditation offered up a different answer.

The thing about intuitive sensings is that what they tell us is often not what we want to hear. Sometimes, it's the opposite of what we want to hear. That's what happened that morning when I heard, "Hit the road."

Intuitive sensings show up different ways for different people; sometimes, in different ways on different days. When I say I "heard," I didn't hear a voice. I don't hear voices. Rather, my intuition speaks to me with what I can only describe as an "inner knowingness," a kind of certainty that defies logic — that "supra-logic" that Robert Graves described.

Because intuition often doesn't make conventional sense, it isn't always easy for me to trust. Still, I do my best to do what Albert Einstein suggests, to "accept intuition as fact," and act accordingly. It's why my memoir is titled *Acts of Surrender*.

When I heard "hit the road," I knew what was being asked of me, because it was the third time in twenty-two years I was intuiting it. On the two previous occasions, both at pivotal moments in my life, that "highest wisdom" directed me to rid myself of most of what I owned, get in the car and see where it took me.

The first, in 1997, carried me from Toronto through ten US states before dropping me three months later in Sedona, Arizona, where my life changed more radically than I could ever have imagined possible.

The second lasted thirty-three months — from late 2004 to late 2007. That odyssey carried me coast-to-coast through more than thirty states and ultimately landed me in Albuquerque, New Mexico for yet more transformation.

In 1997 I had abundant savings and stellar credit. And if my 2004 odyssey launched with a much shakier financial foundation, the public events and private sessions I facilitated while on the road handily (though not always stresslessly) kept me afloat.

I had no comparable resources when I pulled out of Portland on May 28, 2019. Between the cash I had raised from selling what little I owned and my remaining credit, I figured I could last a few weeks. Maybe.

Yet as shaky as my faith was that day, I knew that trusting my intuition was my only option: I would drive east out of Portland and see where the road carried me.

It carried me all the way to the Mississippi and through more than a dozen states, some multiple times, before landing me three months later in a *Groundhog Day*-like reprise of my 1997 journey, back in Sedona.

How did I manage for ninety days on fourteen days' resources? If you're familiar with the story of the Jewish festival of Hanukkah, it was something like that. In the Hanukkah story, when the Syrians who had conquered Israel and outlawed Judaism were finally overthrown and the Temple in Jerusalem rededicated, the priests could find only enough sacred oil to keep the menorah lit for a single day. The miracle of Hanukkah is that the oil lasted until more could be found, for eight days.

My miracle was equally dramatic. Somehow, the necessary resources manifested to keep me going. And somehow, I managed to continue to trust my intuition, even as many urged me to "just park yourself somewhere and get a job."

The most dramatic series of miracles occurred once I arrived in Sedona and committed to staying, although that made no logical sense. If I couldn't support myself in Portland, how would I manage in equally expensive Sedona?

I not only managed, I thrived — against all conventional logic. How? By doing my best to listen to the voice of my heart, still the voice of my fear and surrender to my highest wisdom, my intuition.

It's how I live. It's how I edit. It's how I write.

6. 12½ Secrets to Whole-Brain Editing

> The writer who possesses the creative gift owns something of which he is not always master — something that at times strangely wills and works for itself.
> CHARLOTTE BRONTË

> Only when he no longer knows what he is doing does the painter do good things.
> EDGAR DEGAS

1. There Are No Rules

2. Be True to Your Vision

3. Trust Your Intuition

4. Suspend Judgment

5. Strive for Excellence, Not Perfection

6. Respect All Your Drafts

7. Talk to Your Story

8. Read Aloud, and Listen

9. Read, Anything and Everything

10. Take Your Time

11. Don't Obsess

12. Be the Writer You Are

12½. Be True to Your Vision

The Only Rule That Matters

Just as there is no single right or wrong way to write your book, script, essay, poem, short story or other project, there is no single right or wrong way to edit it that is guaranteed to work for you every time. There is only the way that works for you *today*.

I emphasize "today" because what works for you in revising one project may not always work on the next. So, be open, be flexible and remember that...

Secret #1
There Are No Rules

When it comes to any sort of creative endeavor, there never are rules. There never can be rules. Why not? Because if you're following someone else's rules, you're doing what has been done before, not blazing new trails...which is what creativity is all about.

I'm not talking about the rules of grammar and punctuation, of course, although even those are rarely fixed. There are infinite variations in what is considered acceptable — not only from one language and country to the next but from one publishing house to the next.

Take the Oxford comma, for example, sometimes called the "serial comma," which places a comma before the "and" in a list: *She bought sugar, flour, and eggs.* Although it is more common in the UK than in North America, no rule says you can't use it in the US and Canada. Whatever your preferences — be it Oxford comma-related or otherwise — do your best to be consistent. (See Tip #12 in Section 7, "My Top Twenty Revision Tips.")

Even when you are combing your story for the "Thirty-Three Words and Phrases That Weaken Your Writing" (Section 8), there are no absolutes. Run my recommendations through the filter of your discernment, and remember that your only goal throughout the revision journey is to be true to the spirit and essence of your work and to make your writing as clear and evocative as possible for your readers. Spelling, punctuation, grammar and usage exist to support that goal, not to subvert it.

Nor am I talking about submission requirements and industry standards. When it's time to submit your final draft to a publisher, agent or producer, be aware not only of relevant industry standards (especially strict when it comes to screenplays) but of your intended recipients' submission requirements (generally listed on their website or in online or printed directories like *Writer's Market*). Be aware of them...and meet them. That isn't a rule; it's common sense.

Those submission requirements may call for a particular font, point size or margin setting. They may demand specific spacing. Or they may insist that you include certain elements with your query (e.g. a sample chapter, a synopsis, an outline, your bio and/or a marketing plan). However unreasonable some of those requirements might seem to you, don't ignore them. Publishers, agents and producers receive hundreds of submissions a week. To ensure that yours is at least considered, give them what they ask for.

When I say there are no rules, I'm talking mainly about the revision *process*. My suggestions, particularly those in Section 12 ("Working with Your Drafts") are only that: suggestions. In the end, whatever process transforms the chaos of your early drafts into something readers can't put down is the right process for you. There are no rules.

"The Missing Piece"

When one of the participants at a recent revision workshop of mine identified herself as a technical editor with more than thirty years' experience, I wondered silently why she was there. What use, I asked myself, would a technical editor have with concepts like vision and vision statements?

I watched her closely her through the workshop, half expecting her to challenge me and dismiss my approach...maybe to walk out.

Instead, she acknowledged each of my major points by nodding in agreement, and when, toward the end of the workshop, she crafted her first-ever vision statement, she exclaimed, *"This* is the missing piece!"

When it comes to editing, vision *is* the missing piece, the one never talked about in traditional editing books and classes. Yet, if you lack an overarching vision for your work, how can you know what belongs and what doesn't?

Secret #2
Be True to Your Vision

As you reread your work through as many drafts as your project demands, watch for words, phrases, sentences, scenes or chapters that detract from the essence of your story, that dilute your theme, that weaken your vision. Are there characters who get in the way of that vision? Are there lines of dialogue that conflict with that vision? Are there anecdotes, illustrations or examples that diverge from that vision? Either remove them (see Tip #14 in Section 7) or rework them in a way that illuminates your vision instead of clouding it.

Now is a good time to revisit the vision statement you created in Section 4 or to craft one if you haven't yet done so. Your vision statement will always help you to stay aligned with the true heart of your work, not only in your first draft but all the way to your final draft and beyond.

Try This

Creating a vision statement can be as simple as getting into a meditative space and writing on the Muse Stream from the phrase "My vision for ['title of project' or 'my writing'] is..." Or allow your work to speak about itself, writing on the Muse Stream from a phrase like "I am ['title of project']. I am about..." Or use the "Quick Visioning Meditation" that follows Secret #12½ at the end of this section.

Whatever your choice, allow to come whatever comes, whether it speaks in metaphor, in general terms or with the most specific of detail, and let it guide you as you move forward with your revisions.

How Does It Feel?

Don't rely solely on the logical, detail-oriented side of your brain when you edit. Using your whole brain and body will allow you to see beyond obvious errors and to correct more than surface issues.

Does a sentence, paragraph or chapter not *feel* right?

Does some elusive something about part of your story feel "off" in some way you can't easily identify?

Is there some component of your draft that seems as though it doesn't belong?

Do you have a nagging sensation that something is missing?

Does something else feel out of whack?

Trust those feelings, whether they pop into your head or you feel them somewhere in your body. Yes, in your body. Tickles, tingles, prickles, "butterflies," even sudden aches or pains can signal that something needs a second look, can raise or eliminate a doubt or can indicate that something is particularly powerful.

When I was working on *The MoonQuest*, there were two nightmarish scenes that I spent the entire revision process wishing I could delete. Yet without understanding why, I knew they were somehow integral to the story. More than that, every time I reread them, I felt a stirring in my gut that seemed to validate that sensing.

It wasn't until a year after the book's release that I grasped their importance. To be honest, their importance had to be explained to me — by a reader who was teaching a class based on the book.

"*The MoonQuest* is a story about the power of storytelling," he explained patiently, as if to someone who had never read the book, let alone written it. "It's a story about what is destroyed when we're prevented from telling our stories and about the healing that occurs when we break through the silence and share those stories with each other."

Of course!

My conscious mind hadn't been able to see it because my conscious mind had been too busy being disturbed by the violent content of those scenes. My unconscious mind, however, knew. And it stopped me from censoring myself.

Secret #3
Trust Your Intuition

The more you trust what you feel and sense, the more your intuitive mind will keep you aligned with your work's highest purpose and prevent you from stripping the heart from your work. At the same time it will not only alert you to problems but offer you solutions.

Your intuition will never lead you astray. It is the voice of your vision and the voice of your story.

Taming Your Inner Critic

The part of me that wanted to delete those two *MoonQuest* scenes was my inner critic. It needled me throughout the revision process. From draft to draft, every time I reached that chapter, it would whisper, "Those scenes are crap. Cut them." When that didn't convince me, it would try this: "Those scenes are too different from the rest of the story. They don't fit in. Cut them."

Yet my inner critic's concerns had nothing to do with the quality of my writing or the suitability of those scenes. Rather, my inner critic was taking proactive measures to protect me.

You see, days after I wrote that pair of scenes, I took them to an open mic night at the small-town cafe near where I was then living. The normally attentive audience seemed more hushed than usual through my reading. Or was it shock?

At the end of the evening, a young man came up to me to offer feedback. "Don't you think it was too—" He stopped, struggling for words. "Relentless?"

Thanks to that young man, I had already faced judgment because of those scenes. Why, my inner critic was asking, would I want to open myself to more by including them in the final draft? Wouldn't it be safer to remove them?

Our inner critic — and all creative artists have vigorous inner critics — views the world in stark black-and-white terms. Our writing is good or bad, safe or unsafe. Our inner critic rules the world of our work with the bluntness of a judge's gavel, condemning all or part of it as "unacceptable" or sparing it with a grudging "pass."

Heartful revision, however, is about discernment not judgment.

Discernment is a more delicate tool. Discernment is a marriage of intuition and intellect, a blend of right and left brain, a meld of heart and mind.

Judgment doesn't create excellence (see Secret #5). Discernment does.

SECRET #4
SUSPEND JUDGMENT

Suspend judgment. Expel it altogether. Breathe it out with one forced-air breath and let it evaporate, dissipate and disappear. Now, breathe in discernment. Discern what is powerful about your writing as well as what is weak. Discern what is strong in your writing as well as what needs work.

Notice your judgment but don't give in to it. And do your best to not let it get in the way of your editing.

Feeling judgmental? The following guided meditation will help you edit with more clarity and less judgment.

Taming Your Inner Critic: A Guided Meditation

Allow at least 30 minutes for this meditation and for any journaling experiences that flow from it.

My professional recording of a version of this meditation is available for download or streaming as part "The Voice of the Muse Companion: Guided Meditations for Writers." See "Guided Meditations" in Section 1 to find out how to access the recording, as well as for tips on how best to use this book's meditations.

Sit or lie in a comfortable position. Close your eyes and take a few deep breaths. Let yourself relax. Feel yourself relax on your breath.

Now, let your shoulders drop...and drop some more. And some more. And some more.

Breathe deeply and fully, feeling the breath fill not only your lungs and abdomen but your entire body — from head to toes and back again.

And again.

And again.

Feel the breath cleanse you. Feel it dissolve your fears, your anxiety, your stress. Feel it strengthen you, empower you. Feel it protect you, keep you safe. Feel it open your heart. Feel it open your mind.

There have been times in your life when you have been criticized, times in your life when you have been judged. Of course there have. We have all had those experiences. As children. As adolescents. As adults.

Sometimes, the experience rolled off us painlessly. Sometimes, it felt excruciatingly cruel. Sometimes, we forged ahead in spite of it. Sometimes, it shut us down.

It's all normal, all perfect, all part of the human experience. And as with all human experience, we can choose how to react or respond, we can choose how each instance will affect us.

Don't judge how you have reacted or responded in the past. Simply be aware and continue breathing. Fully. Deeply. Allow your breath to once again dissolve any stress or anxiety triggered by unpleasant memories.

Know that you are safe.

Protected.

Free from harm of any sort.

From that place of relaxed breathing, from that place of safety, call into your mind, heart and/or consciousness your harshest critic. Perhaps it's someone in your past or present life. A teacher. A parent. A sibling. Another relative. A friend. A school or neighborhood bully. A boss, professional colleague or coworker.

Feel whatever charge you feel around this individual, and breathe. Feel whatever charge you feel around this individual and let that feeling dissolve on your breath.

Now, let that critic transform into some kind of image, something that represents that critic, that stands in for that critic. A symbol. A metaphor. Perhaps it's an animal. Perhaps it's a reptile or a mythical beast. Perhaps it's another human form or another type of form altogether. Perhaps it's a color or shape. Or perhaps it doesn't change form at all.

Let it be what it is and know that however it shows up is perfect in this moment. Regardless of how it shows up, see it not as an external critic but as an internalized aspect of you, ready to engage with you.

Whatever it is, whoever it is, however it is, greet it and begin a dialogue with it. Have a conversation with it. Engage with it.

Write this dialogue as it occurs or let it emerge silently in your heart.

In the first part of your conversation, ask your critic why it judged you so cruelly, what provoked its behavior, what it was afraid of.

If this is an ongoing situation, frame your questions in the present tense.

Listen with an open heart. Respond with an open heart. Allow compassion. Allow understanding. Allow forgiveness. Allow love.

Give yourself thirty seconds of clock time for this part of the experience. Or pause the recording until you are ready to continue.

Be aware that if you are experiencing judgment, you are likely expressing judgment in certain areas of your life. Have compassion for yourself for your judgments. Be understanding. Be forgiving. Be loving. Be open. Be respectful. Toward yourself.

Commit as well to directing those same attitudes toward others, toward anyone you are tempted to criticize harshly.

Now, as you return to the conversation with your critic, ask it how the two of you can work together from this moment forward to bring your writing and your life to their fullest, most magnificent potential. Ask it how it can assist you, productively and discerningly, as you shape, polish and refine your work.

Converse. Discuss. Negotiate. Dialogue. Engage. Silently or in writing.

Again, be loving and compassionate. Be understanding and forgiving. Be respectful. Be open.

Allow another thirty seconds of clock time for this part of the experience. Or, again, pause the recording until you're ready to continue.

Now it is time to bring your encounter to a close. Thank this aspect of yourself for its assistance, for its openness, for its willingness to transform. And commit to this new partnership. Commit, too, to the spirit of cooperation the two of you have now forged in love and mutual respect.

When you feel complete, journal about your experiences and discoveries. Use all your senses to paint a picture in words of your new awareness, your renewed creative power and your heightened ability to be discerning.

When you're finished journaling, remember to read your words from a place of love, openness and non-judgment. Remember your commitment to partnership and cooperation. And as you return to revision work on your story, remember to read those words, too, from a place of love, openness and non-judgment. From a heartful place. From a place of discernment.

Embrace Imperfection

Whether in writing or in life, many of us are addicted to perfectionism. Being perfect, we believe, guarantees that we will never be criticized, judged, rejected or humiliated. Being perfect means fewer drafts and revisions. Being perfect means instant success and worldwide fame.

Okay, so a Pulitzer Prize or an Oscar may not happen...at least not right away. But being perfect is, well, a good thing to be. Isn't it?

It might be if it were possible. It isn't. No matter how hard you try and how many drafts you churn out, your writing will never achieve perfection. Never.

Not ever.

Your work may be excellent, accomplished, creative and insightful. It may be innovative and compelling. It may be brilliant. But perfect? Not possible.

It's not possible because when we translate an idea or concept into language, we're taking something infinite (energy) and dynamic (neural impulses) and converting it into something finite (language) and static (squiggles on a page or pixels on a screen). The resulting "translation" can never be more than approximate.

Can you describe the sunset you experienced last night in words that will accurately and precisely convey to me every shade and nuance of what you saw and felt? Can you write a scene that reproduces the exact emotions you experienced when your child was born, when you got married or when a loved one died?

Of course you can't. Nor would I want you to. As a reader I want to be free to have my experience of your sunset and your emotions, and my experience cannot be a faultless replica of yours, colored as it must be by my life and background. Until we can somehow link your writer-brain directly to my reader-brain, that translation will remain imprecise and imperfect.

In the end, perfection is not possible in any creative endeavor. It's not possible in any human endeavor. It's simply not possible. As Salvador Dali cautioned, "Have no fear of perfection, you'll never reach it."

Secret #5
Strive for Excellence, Not Perfection

If perfection is elusive, excellence is not. Do your best from one draft to the next to translate your vision onto the pages of your work. But don't beat yourself up or trash your drafts because they aren't perfect. Accept the inherent imperfection that is the perfection of all creative enterprise, and when you have done the best you can, let it go and move on to your next project.

Management consultant Edwin Bliss put it best when he said, "There's a difference between striving for excellence and striving for perfection. The first is attainable, gratifying and healthy. The second is often unattainable, frustrating and neurotic."

No Word (or Draft) Is Ever Wasted

It is easy to dismiss aspects of the journey toward a final draft as pointless...to judge those words, sentences, scenes and chapters that end up on the cutting room floor as having been unnecessary...to judge ourselves for having wasted time, effort and energy in writing them.

As I noted in "Language Matters" (Section 3), there can be no wasted time, effort or energy in the creative process. Each word, sentence, scene and chapter you write serves an essential purpose: Each is a necessary paving stone on the road to your final draft.

SECRET #6
RESPECT ALL YOUR DRAFTS

Treat each draft of your story as you would your child — with love and without judgment. Just as you gently, sometimes firmly, guide your children toward the fulfillment of their unique destinies, guide your work with that same spirit of respect — for yourself as its creator as well as for your creation, which has its own vision and imperative.

Recognize that no word written and no draft composed is ever wasted. Each word and each draft carry you to the next...to the next...to the next...and, ultimately, not only to the final word of the final draft of this story, but to the first word of the first draft of your next story.

Respect your first draft. Respect all your drafts, without being a slave to any of them. Allow your work to grow, change and mature. And allow yourself to grow, change and mature with it.

HERE'S A SUGGESTION

Recycle any favorite aspects of a particular draft that you feel you must cut by creating an "outtakes" folder. Use the folder's contents to trigger ideas for new stories, in planned future projects or to launch Muse Stream writing exercises.

¶ *See also Revision Tip #14 in "My Top Twenty Revision Tips," Section 7.*

Your Story Is Smarter Than You Are

If I have learned anything through my decades of writing, it's that my stories are smarter than I am. Infinitely smarter. Always.

Each of my books and screenplays has surprised me, and each has been more imaginative, more compelling, more readable, more inspiring, more memorable and/or more entertaining because in allowing myself to be surprised, I surrendered to that story's superior wisdom — in both the writing of it and the editing of it.

Your story knows itself better than you ever will. Your story knows its ideal form, shape and structure. Your story knows its characters, situations, conflicts and settings. Your story knows its theme. Your story knows its thesis and arguments. Your story probably also knows its ultimate destination and fate.

If it knows all that, and I promise you it does, it also knows not only where your narrative, plot, descriptions and/or characterizations have gone astray but how best to rework them to more closely resemble its spirit and essence.

As you move from draft to draft, sit in the silence with your story. Listen for its wisdom and guidance. Talk to it.

Secret #7

Talk to Your Story

If your stories are smarter than you are and your characters know themselves better than you ever will, why not ask them what they need from you...what you need from them.

How do you talk to your stories and, where relevant, your characters? By using a technique I call "meditative dialogue" to enter into a "conversation" with the essence and spirit of your writing project. You did something similar in the "Taming Your Inner Critic" meditation in Secret #4.

The meditative journey that follows will guide you through the experience, but if you don't have thirty minutes to spare and you need immediate answers, turn the page for the quick version.

Continue to turn to meditative dialogue all the way through the revision process and your story will tell you what is missing from your script or manuscript and what needs refining. Listen with your heart and trust what you hear — in terms of content, shape, theme, format, language and structure.

Remember: Your story knows best, through every stage of your journey together.

Talk to Your Story: A Meditative Journey

Allow at least 30 minutes for this meditation and for any journaling experiences that flow from it.

See "Guided Meditations" in Section 1 for tips on how best to use this book's meditations.

Have pen and paper, tablet or laptop handy, or sit as comfortably as you can at your desk or computer table.

Settle into a physical, emotional and spiritual state of stillness. If you have a meditation practice, do whatever you normally do to get into a receptive space. If not, close your eyes and sit quietly, focusing on your breath to quiet your mind.

Use music, aromatherapy, crystals, yoga or ritual if you find any or all of these to be helpful. You can also use the "Listen to Your Heart" meditation in Section 5 or the shorter "You Are a Writer" meditation in Section 16 to relax you and help get you into a receptive space for this experience.

If, in the end, you are unable to still your mind, don't worry about it. Writing your mind-chatter will give it voice and, ultimately, silence it.

Write the first thought about your writing project that comes to mind. It can be about your vision for the project, about the finished project, about a particular draft or about an element of the current draft. It can relate to a doubt or concern. It can be a question or feeling.

It can be a statement of praise or complaint. It can be the voice of your inner critic, of your fear or of your inner child. It can be nattering mind noise.

Whatever it is, write your side of the conversation, then let a response emerge spontaneously onto the page. Don't search your mind for an answer. Don't think about an answer. *Let* the answer.

The key, in both sides of your conversation, is to write on the Muse Stream — without stopping, without thinking, without correcting spelling, punctuation or grammar and, most particularly, without censoring or second-guessing. In doing so, you will write through and past any judgment or fear and you will discover what you already knew about your story or your concerns but didn't know you knew.

Continue your dialogue for as long as you feel the need to and then a little longer. The wisest words and deepest truths often emerge after we think we're finished.

If you get stuck, revisit the tips at the end of Section 4's "The Muse Stream."

TRY THIS

Adapt this exercise to "interview" your characters if you're writing script or prose fiction.

Talk to Your Story: A Quick Meditation

Get yourself into a meditative space and listen. Listen for the voice of your story or for the voices of your characters and trust what you hear. The more you practice this technique, the more comfortable you will feel asking specific questions of your story and its characters and the easier it will be to hear their answers and trust them.

Making Music

"To me," Truman Capote said, "the greatest pleasure of writing is not what it's about, but the music the words make."

All language is music. And one of the best ways to attune to the music of language is to read aloud.

Secret #8

Read Aloud, and Listen

As you read aloud, listen for that music...or for where it's missing. Note that individual forms, genres and media communicate best with particular kinds of music. This can be equally true with different chapters and scenes in the same work. Each of your characters, if you're writing fiction or script, also speaks with a distinctive rhythm and cadence, which is easiest to hear when you act it out. (See "Refining Your Dialogue," Section 9.)

When you read aloud and *listen*, you hear what works and what doesn't — sometimes consciously, often intuitively. You notice where you stumble. You notice where flow fails, where suspense doesn't build, where your writing falls flat.

When you read aloud, you notice where sentences sound too much alike or where sentence length or style doesn't support a scene or a desired emotion. Short, simple sentences, for example, can build suspense. Longer sentences slow the reader to a more leisurely pace. Know the effect you want and, as you revise, adjust your sentences accordingly.

When you read aloud, you spot where a word is in the wrong place, where you have used the wrong word or where you have unintentionally missed or repeated a word. You will even spot spelling and punctuation errors because reading aloud forces you to read more slowly and more closely and to not skim over or skip words.

You will want to read your work silently as well, of course. But especially at the beginning and each time you make major changes, your voice will tell you where you have strayed off course.

Perhaps reading aloud works so well because it takes us back not only to childhood bedtime stories but to that deep storytelling past we all carry as part of our emotional DNA. In fact it's such a powerful tool that I not only read aloud when I'm revising, I often read aloud as I'm writing, which can get me some pretty strange looks in cafes and other public places!

¶ *See also Tip #10 in "My Top Twenty Revision Tips," Section 7.*

The Power of Osmosis

Osmosis is one of the most powerful learning tools available to the human heart and mind. When you read great writing, you absorb the writer's craft and technique. You sense at an intuitive level what works and what doesn't — without having to know or understand how or why...without needing to analyze, parse or dissect...without trying to figure anything out. You *know*, and that knowingness finds its way into your writing and rewriting, effortlessly and often unconsciously.

SECRET #9
READ, ANYTHING AND EVERYTHING

Form and genre don't matter. Topic doesn't matter. What matters is that you read good writing by accomplished writers. "A lot of what I know," says film director Peter Bogdanovich, "I learned through osmosis."

Savor the Journey

It's human nature to prefer to rush the journey from first to final draft. It's human nature to focus on the moment of completion rather than on the journey that gets us there.

Creativity, however, is not a cookie-cutting manufacturing mechanism that stamps out instant finished stories. Creativity is more like a Rube Goldberg contraption, a convoluted, time-consuming process that makes little sense to our logical minds. It's a relationship — with our Muse and our writing project, a relationship that may also make little conventional sense and that, to guarantee a successful outcome, may require more time and drafts than we might prefer.

Unless you're facing a rigid deadline, let your work sit quietly for a time before you launch into revision. Set your work aside between drafts as well. That time could be a day, a week, a month or six months. And it could be longer or shorter from one piece of work to the next and from one draft to the next.

The key is to give you and your work the space and distance that allow you to approach it heartfully, objectively, discerningly and with the clear perspective of a fresh eye.

If you can't help but judge what you've written or the edits you have made, wait until you're able to approach each new draft from a place of wisdom and perception, not from one of self-criticism and self-doubt.

Once you begin a new draft, don't rush the process. Your work deserves your full attention and consideration. Be thorough without being obsessive and take whatever time each draft demands of you.

SECRET #10

TAKE YOUR TIME

No task was ever performed more effectively by rushing through it.

Revision is a delicate process. Don't put your finished work — and perhaps your reputation — at risk with careless and reckless speed. Respect yourself and your work (Secret #6) by taking your time with each draft and between drafts.

Don't Be Like Oscar Wilde

"I was working on the proof of one of my poems all morning, and took out a comma," Oscar Wilde once wrote. "In the afternoon I put it back again."

Through every stage of your revision experience, you will discover infinite opportunities to obsess about one thing or another. Don't do it.

SECRET #11

DON'T OBSESS

Your Best Is Good Enough

There will be errors you will miss. There will be errors editors and proofreaders will miss. Regardless of the number of times you read a draft and have it read by others, including by professionals, mistakes will slip through. When you discover them, note them so you can correct future editions. Then let them go.

As I urged with Secret #11, don't obsess. Simply do your best.

Do your best to bring your heart and vision to the page. Do your best to write the words and paint the images that most accurately reflect your dream and intention. As you revise, never hesitate to seek out more forceful and evocative ways to translate your vision onto the page. But remember that translation is an art and that perfection does not exist.

Remember, too, that language can rarely more than approximate emotion and experience. Think of the most wondrous moment in your life and imagine trying to reproduce it in words. You can come close. Yet whatever your mastery of the language, you will not recreate every emotional nuance. And that's okay.

Each draft of your work will teach you, and from each draft you will mature in your art and your craft. Let each draft be what it needs to be. Let each draft be the foundation for your next. Let each piece of writing be what it needs to be. Let each piece of writing be the foundation for your next.

Secret #12
Be the Writer You Are

In case You Forgot...

As you revise your script or manuscript, hold your vision for your story (and your story's vision for you) in your heart and mind, and let that vision guide you as you realign those scenes or chapters that have strayed from center and those words, actions or descriptions that are not true to character.

Secret #12½
Be True to Your Vision

If you haven't already done so, craft a vision statement for your writing. Use the quick meditation that follows or the "Your Vision" meditation in Section 4.

Quick Visioning Meditation

Allow at least 10 minutes for this meditation and for the writing experiences that flow from it.

A version of this guided meditation is included as part of my video workshop, "The Heartful Art of Revision: An Intuitive Guide to Editing." See the "Guided Meditations" chapter in Section 1 to find out how to access the video, as well as for tips on how best to use this book's meditations.

If you have already written a vision statement, let this exercise carry you deeper, to a fresh perspective and to any newly awakened aspects of your vision that this experience kindles.

Close your eyes and relax. Let yourself sink into whatever you're sitting on or lying on and take a deep breath, breathing in to your connection with your Muse or whatever you choose to call your creative spirit.

Breathe out your immediate surroundings and all distractions they could inject into your space.

Again, breathe in to your creative source, and feel yourself fill with that energy, that spirit, that openness. And as you breathe out, breathe out all fear and all anxieties.

Let your in-breath carry you deep into your heart, the source of all your stories. And as you breathe out, breathe out all worries, all stress, all strain.

If you have a project you're working on, let your breath carry you into a place of profound connection with it, a place of union with it, a place where you and it are one.

Alternatively, let your breath carry you into a place of profound connection with your creatorship, a place of union with it, a place where you and it are one.

As you breathe out, let go all preconceptions, all expectations, all shoulds and musts about your writing project or about your writerly self.

Allow yourself to surrender to what your writing project is, not what you think it ought to be. Allow yourself to surrender to the writer you are in your deepest core, not the writer you think you are or should be.

Surrender to that. Breathe into that. Be one with that.

Whether this experience is connecting you with an individual project or with the core of your writerly self, let your next breath open your heart and mind to its vision for itself...to its vision for you.

This experience is not about crafting a vision statement from your conscious mind. It's about letting your work and your deepest creative self speak to you through your heart...through your unconscious mind.

So let your breath carry you there. This breath...and now this breath...and now this breath.

In a moment, I am going to ask you to open your eyes and write on the Muse Stream from a phrase I am going to give you. This phrase will be an expression of your vision for your work or of your vision for yourself. Again, not a conscious expression. A deeper, truer, fuller expression.

Don't be attached to the phrase. If some other way of expressing your vision comes to you, go with that.

Regardless, go wherever the Muse Stream takes you...even if it appears to be taking you off course.

Don't judge what comes. Don't actively choose what to write or where to go with it. Let it carry you where you need to go. Writing on the Muse Stream is always about letting and allowing. Writing on the Muse Stream is always about surrender.

So allow to come whatever comes. The length doesn't matter. The form and language don't matter. Your conscious mind's understanding of what you have written doesn't matter.

What matters is that, at some level, you and your creation sing the same song and that that harmony supports you as you refine and enrich your writing.

So once again be conscious of your breath...of your physical body, of the physical space you now occupy, as you allow your breath to return you to full awareness.

And when you feel ready, taking all the time you need, gently open your eyes and be fully present, ready to write on the Muse Stream from this phrase:

My vision for ["my writing project" or "myself as the writer I am"] is...

If you know your project's title or working title, include it. If you don't, include its form — for example, "my book" or "my poem" or "my script." If you're not yet clear on its form, use the phrase "my writing project."

My vision for ["my writing project" or "myself as the writer I am"] is...

Follow the words where they take you, and let your pen pull your hand across the page as you to surrender to the journey...as you surrender to your vision.

7. My Top Twenty Revision Tips

So the writer who breeds more words than he needs,
is making a chore for the reader who reads.
DR. SEUSS

I know that a scene is good when I feel my heart beat faster...
EMIR KUSTURICA

1. Break Free of Your Crutches

2. Make Friends with a Thesaurus

3. Convert Your Clichés

4. Get Active (Unless It's Better to Stay Passive)

5. Do More Showing Than Telling

6. Don't Overexplain

7. Don't Under-Explain

8. Be Specific

9. Paint Pictures with Your Words

10. Let Your Language Sing

11. Clear up Ambiguities

12. Clean up Inconsistencies

13. Eliminate Redundancy

14. Free Your Favorites

15. Write the Right Word

16. Double-Check Your Facts and Figures

17. Curb Your Exclamations

18. Be Typographical

19. Proofread

20. Be True to Your Vision

1. Break Free of Your Crutches

In his 2017 book *Nabokov's Favorite Word Is Mauve: What the Numbers Reveal About the Classics, Bestsellers, and Our Own Writing*, journalist Ben Blatt takes us on a statistical journey through classic, bestselling, Pulitzer Prize-winning and amateur fiction and finds, among other surprisingly entertaining results, that professional and award-winning authors employ considerably fewer "-ly" adverbs than do amateurs.

Ernest Hemingway, known for his spare use of language, used only eighty "-ly" adverbs per ten thousand words. Yet even Mark Twain and John Steinbeck clocked in at fewer than ninety, with Kurt Vonnegut, John Updike, Salman Rushdie and Stephen King all hovering around a hundred. Yet those numbers are high, according to Blatt, who found that between sixty and eighty percent of books considered "great" use fewer than fifty adverbs per ten thousand words.

Does that mean that all adverbs are bad and ought to be avoided? Of course not. No rules, remember? However, adjectives as well as adverbs can weaken your writing when you use them as crutches to prop up sickly nouns and verbs.

Which example tells you more about Katherine's speed? "She walked slowly" or "she ambled"? Depending on Katherine's purpose, you could also have her stroll, saunter or wander to her destination, assuming she has one. "Wander," for instance, would suggest no fixed or immediate destination, something that "slowly" does not, at least not in this context.

If you write "Brad drove an old car," we can't know whether Brad was driving a rare 1935 Duesenberg SSJ (once owned by Gary Coper and which sold at auction for $22 million) or a rust bucket he paid to have towed to a junkyard. (See also Tips #8 and 9.) Here, "old" only barely modifies "car."

In this example, a weak adjective attempts to hold up a second, equally weak adjective: "Peter was quite happy." "Quite happy" doesn't reveal much about Peter's mood. Perhaps Peter was ecstatic or elated. Perhaps he was jubilant or contented. Perhaps he was overjoyed or triumphant. When "quite" is present, what follows it is often a rickety noun. That's also true of "very," "abnormally," "a bit" and "extremely." (See also "Thirty-Three Words and Phrases That Weaken Your Writing" and "Twenty-Five Damn Good Replacements for 'Very'" in Section 8.)

As you revise your work, seek out evocative verbs and nouns that stand on their own power and break free of those crutches. Even when adverbs and adjectives help you paint a more vibrant picture, seek out expressive ones and pair them with forceful nouns and dynamic verbs for more potent and descriptive writing.

Need help finding nouns and verbs (and adjectives and adverbs) to enliven and strengthen your narrative? That's what Tip #2 is all about.

2. Make Friends with a Thesaurus

Stephen King is often misquoted on thesaurus use. It's true he once insisted that the best place for a thesaurus is "in the wastebasket." But he was referring to first drafts, not to the revision process.

Use a thesaurus (in revision, *not* while writing) to find words that eloquently and effectively reflect your intent. Words like "beautiful," "nice" and "interesting," for example, convey nothing to your reader. Search your thesaurus for adjectives that more accurately communicate what you're seeking to describe and that more effectively express your vision, or look for nouns that eliminate the need for an adjective. The same is true for verbs and adverbs.

Note that not all synonyms are created equal. Understand the subtleties of a potential replacement's meaning before using it. Take the word "potential" in the previous sentence. The *Oxford American Writer's Thesaurus* offers the following alternatives: "possible, likely, prospective, future, probable, budding, in the making; latent, embryonic, developing, dormant, inherent, unrealized, undeveloped." Synonyms like "possible" or "prospective" could work in the context of that sentence; "embryonic," "dormant" and "unrealized" would make no sense.

And don't show off: Big words are rarely better. Obscure words are never better. (See "Keep it Simple...but Not Too Simple," Section 8.)

As with any friendship, don't abuse your relationship. Use your thesaurus as a collaborator not as a crutch.

3. Convert Your Clichés

Clichéd writing is lazy writing. Clichéd writing is impotent writing. Clichéd writing is dull.

Have you used any of the following in your story?

- *All's fair in love and war*
- *Back in the saddle*
- *Chip off the old block*
- *Dead as a doornail*
- *Easy as pie*
- *Fit to be tied*
- *Good as gold*
- *In the nick of time*
- *Light at the end of the tunnel*
- *Like a kid in a candy store*
- *No time like the present*
- *Play your cards right*
- *Plenty of fish in the sea*
- *Thick as thieves*
- *Time heals all wounds*
- *Wakeup call*

Avoid them like the plague. (Avoid that cliché too!)

Remember Ben Blatt? He also looked at clichés in *Nabokov's Favorite Word Is Mauve* and found that the best writers use them sparingly. Jane Austen, for example, used a mere forty-five per hundred thousand words; J.R.R. Tolkien used seventy-three per hundred thousand. Among contemporary authors, Neil Gaiman was a standout with only ninety-two per hundred thousand.

As you go back over your script or manuscript, look for platitudes, hackneyed phrases and overused metaphors like the ones I have listed and replace them with original writing that provokes, astounds and astonishes.

Here's an exception: Does one of your characters speak in clichés as part of his or her natural speech pattern? If so, leave enough of those clichés intact to communicate the character's tendency but not so many that readers will struggle with it. (See also "The Seven Elements of Authentic Dialogue" in Section 9.)

4. Get Active (unless It's Better to Stay Passive)

When you write with the active voice, the subject of your sentence performs the action: "The dog bit Jeremy." Here, the dog is the subject; Jeremy is the object.

The active voice is simpler and more direct than the passive voice. The active voice...

- emphasizes the actor over the action
- makes it clears who is responsible for the action; in other words, who deserves credit or blame
- is more compact and concise
- more closely resembles spoken language
- is easier to read than the passive voice
- is more direct, more impactful and, according to studies, more memorable

With the passive voice, the subject receives the action: "Janet was bitten by the dog." Here, Janet is the subject.

The passive voice tends to be vague, awkward, stilted and wordy. It can also obscure responsibility for the action it describes by removing its source, which is why it is often used by politicians and in large bureaucracies. For example, "Mistakes were made." In this sentence, the perpetrator of those mistakes is never revealed.

At the same time, the passive voice has its uses. The passive voice...

- creates an aura of mystery: "The jewels were stolen"
- focuses on the unknown: "The major was killed"

The passive voice is also more objective, in that it removes the author's opinions from a conclusion and disregards extraneous information — "The blood was sampled" (by whom is irrelevant). As well, it carries an air of objectivity that can be helpful in scientific and academic writing because it removes the author from a study's conclusion: "The results were reviewed" or "It was found that pigs can fly."

TRY THIS

Can you transform these three passive sentences into active ones? Suggested solutions are in the footnote at the bottom of the page.[1]

1. Dinner was served by their butler.
2. My car was hit from behind by my neighbor's motorcycle.
3. A retired minister was conscripted by Mary to perform the marriage ceremony.

---

[1] 1. Their butler served dinner.
2. My neighbor's motorcycle smashed into the back of my car.
3. Mary conscripted a retired minister to perform the marriage ceremony.

5. Do More Showing Than Telling

Show, don't tell. This piece of writing advice is repeated so often it's almost a cliché. What does it mean?

Perhaps the best explanation is this quote attributed to Russian playwright Anton Chekhov: "Don't tell me the moon is shining; show me the glint of light on broken glass."

In other words, use action, detail, dialogue and description to spark your reader's imagination.

As you revise, transform as many "shows" as appropriate into "tells." Don't tell me Jack is a cheap bastard. Show him being a cheap bastard. Don't tell me that Jill is ungrateful. Describe her in a way that communicates her lack of gratitude.

Here are three reasons why it's generally preferable to show:

- "Showing" is more expressive and evocative. "Telling" is often weak, flat and dry.

- "Showing" paints an image in your readers' minds and frees them to experience your story their way, not yours. "Telling" is more controlling; it instructs your readers what to think or believe.

- "Showing" offers readers a visceral and/or emotional experience. "Telling" is more intellectual and abstract.

If it's generally better to show, it's not always bad to tell. "Telling" can be preferable when you are communicating important but nonessential information. For example, when nothing significant occurs on a journey, "showing" could bog the narrative down with unnecessary detail. In that instance, it might be better to move a character from point A to point B with limited or no "showing."

Try This

Can you convert these "tells" into "shows"? I adapted the first from my novel *Sara's Year* and the second from *The Emmeline Papers*. Read how they appear in the two books in the footnote at the bottom of the page.[2]

Although the second example is preferable to something vaguer, like "Jeremy was lonely," the fuller description is more poignant because it shows how he misses her.

1. Stella felt hot.

2. Jeremy missed Emmeline.

---

[2] 1. Stella mopped her glistening forehead with a handkerchief.

2. The radio was playing when Jeremy opened the front door. Since Emmeline's death he had taken to leaving either it or the telly switched on in order that the house not seem so echoingly empty when he returned.

6. Don't Overexplain

What have you overexplained or over-described (possibly because you are being too controlling and don't trust your readers to "get it")? Your readers are smarter, more knowledgeable, more imaginative and more sophisticated than you think.

You don't have to explain everything to them, nor do you need to spell out something that is common knowledge or describe every particular of every situation or every moment of every day. And unless you are writing erotica, it's preferable to avoid presenting sex scenes in graphic, anatomical detail.

As you revise your story, think of how the Impressionists freed viewers to have their own experience of a painting. Give your readers that same space.

7. Don't Under-Explain

What have you *not* explained to your readers? Where have you left gaps in your descriptions, explanations and/or instructions that leave readers flailing? Are there holes in your story or narrative that ought to be filled? Are there steps you have omitted to list or explain? Are you making assumptions based on your intimate knowledge of your topic or of the story, its settings or its players?

Unless you are writing to a specific or knowledgeable audience, your readers may need more description, explanation and/or clarification than you have provided.

Ask yourself the questions your readers will — and answer them.

8. Be Specific

Imagine you're painting a picture or making a movie. What would you want your reader to see and experience? Specifics bring your reader more fully into that picture, into your story, into an experience that becomes theirs.

Now is the time to seek out descriptions that aren't specific enough and develop them.

You have written, "It was a beautiful day." What was beautiful about it? How did it make you or your character feel? What did it smell like? What did it sound like? Describe it. Take your skeletons and add flesh to them. Illuminate your scenes with detail, spirit and emotion, and bring them to life for your readers.

What make and color is the car? What does it smell like? Is the interior cloth or leather? New-looking or worn? Pristine or littered with greasy fast-food cartons? What kind of flowers are in the bouquet? What shapes are the clouds? Is the grass clipped or unruly? Is it green or brown?

What are the colors — of eyes, walls, sunsets, dogs, moods? Are there original ways you can express those colors? By using metaphor? A different point of view? A child's perspective? An inanimate object's perspective?

A single detail about who in your story drives what kind of car, for instance, and how she or he drives it can reveal more about that individual in a few words than several paragraphs of narrative description.

Does he hold the steering wheel in a death grip? Does she chew her fingernails at every traffic light while peering anxiously out the rearview mirror? Is her foot always heavy on the accelerator? Does he creep along the freeway — in the fast lane?

Shrewd use of detail and imagery will immerse readers into the worlds you have created in unrivaled ways.

This is also the time to dilute or delete unnecessary detail. Give your readers the specifics that will bring your story to life, but don't drown them in superfluities.

The key in this as in all things is balance and discernment. Don't use description gratuitously — to show how smart or creative you are or to pad your word count. Use it to reveal character, to add depth and texture. Over-description and petty detail can be as off-putting as not enough. As I mentioned in Tip #6, allow what you describe to most resemble an Impressionist painting — enough color and detail to allow your readers to "connect the dots," but not so hyperreal that it overwhelms them.

Finally, watch for words like *some*times, *some*thing, *some*one, *some*where, *some*what, *some*body and *some*how, which always refer to that which is unknown or unspecified. Unless vagueness is called for — "somebody killed him" — do your best to be specific.

9. Paint Pictures with Your Words

As you reread, revise and rewrite your script or manuscript, look for opportunities to increase or fine-tune your use of imagery. What do things smell and taste like? What do they sound like? What is their texture? Cross senses for more powerful imagery: Ask what the wind tastes like, what the earth sounds like…what someone's face feels like, what the town smells like, what your heartbeat looks like. Engage your senses…and your readers'.

Where possible, paint word pictures that draw on related images. What do I mean by that? In the previous sentence, for example, I chose words like "paint," "pictures," "draw" and "images" to build and reinforce a particular idea. Would it have been as effective had I written, "Use word pictures that tap into related concepts"? You multiply the power of your imagery when you build on linked images to describe something. When one image in the series breaks from the theme, you weaken your overall picture.

As with any other tool, beware of excess. You want to connect your readers with the sensory power of your story; you don't want to overstimulate them. Imagery used wisely and judiciously will always enhance your writing, regardless of its type or genre. Imagery used indiscriminately will only disrupt your flow and bore or overwhelm your readers.

10. Let Your Language Sing

The rhythm, music and flow of your language show up not only in your choice of words and use of imagery but in how you structure your sentences and how you vary sentence length and style. As I noted in Secret #8, a series of short, simple sentences keeps readers in a state of anticipation and impels them to keep reading. Lengthier compound sentences give your reader the space to luxuriate in your prose. The best writing blends sentences of varying lengths and styles.

You needn't parse your sentences and deliberately shuffle their form to create the kind of music I'm talking about. Simply train your ear to listen for the music and trust your intuitive editor to make the necessary adjustments. The best way to listen? Read aloud (Secret #8). A great way to hone your intuition? Read others' work (Secret #9) — not to analyze their style but to absorb, by osmosis, what works and what doesn't.

"I love writing," James Michener said. "I love the swirl and swing of words as they tangle with human emotions." Let your words and sentences swirl...and let your language sing.

11. Clear up Ambiguities

Can your sentence be read two different ways with two distinct meanings? For example: "The boss spoke about sex with Jack." As written, we can't know whether the topic was sex with Jack or whether the boss was talking to Jack and the topic was sex. Rewrite it for clarity. Jack and the boss will be grateful!

Sloppy or improper use of punctuation can also result in ambiguous or unintended meanings. Take this example: "Are you ready to eat, Grandma?" Once you remove the comma, Grandma is no longer being lunched; she *is* lunch.

As you revise, seek out ambiguities, and rewrite — or re-punctuate — for clarity.

12. Clean Up Inconsistencies

In your story, is Jill's dress red on page 112 but blue five pages later? We're talking about the same dress, not a different one.

Has Jack's Toyota Corolla somehow morphed into a Prius without you realizing it?

Does Fred's name become Frank halfway through and Fergus by the final chapter?

Have you changed your mind about Ginger's occupation, nationality or age but forgotten to rewrite earlier chapters to reflect her rejigged identity?

Perhaps you have described the same staircase as having thirteen steps in one section of your account and twenty-three in another. Or maybe the building belonging to the staircase moved across town somewhere in mid-narrative.

Here's another common occurrence: You have added, cut, merged or moved scenes, chapters, illustrations, examples and/or instructions in ways that either create contradictions in your text or affect references and cross-references. Or you have shifted some of the characteristics or experiences of one of your characters to another, peppering your draft with conflicts and inconsistencies.

Books (nonfiction as well as fiction), screenplays, articles and short stories are filled with details that can shift from one scene, chapter, section or draft to the next — sometimes intentionally, often not. When such errors creep into your work, it not only confuses your readers, it can erode your credibility enough to cause them to stop reading.

Through my many drafts of *The MoonQuest*, for example, several characters renamed themselves partway through, sometimes multiple times. Descriptions of certain people and places also underwent frequent changes, as did the unusual spellings of many of my fantasy-world flora and fauna. Reading aloud helped in these situations: I was more likely to notice when something didn't match up when I spoke it.

With my *Sara Stories* novels, which span five decades and involve complicated genealogies, I created a spreadsheet to help me keep track of sometimes complex character details and relationships — within each novel and from one to the next. (Some writing apps include tools and timelines to help you maintain this kind of consistency.)

Conflicts and inconsistencies are inevitable, especially in lengthy scripts and manuscripts. It's your job to weed them out.

13. Eliminate Redundancy

Have you said the same thing more than once, identically or similarly? It could be a description, a piece of dialogue, a tip or a piece of advice. It could be a location or an instruction. It could be an entire scene. There are occasions when repetition — including unintentional repetition — is appropriate, when it serves your work and your readers. More often, though, repetition is superfluous. As you revise your story, remove or rework those instances that don't belong. Also, watch for words you have accidentally repeated repeated. These can be easy to to miss, even when proofreading. As always, reading aloud helps.

14. Free Your Favorites

The sentence you love most, the description you are convinced is unparalleled, the piece of dialogue you consider to be the apex of eloquence, the image you believe to be perfect, the character you know to be flawlessly drawn: These are your favorites, and you may have an unhealthy attachment to them.

View them objectively, from a place of loving detachment. Look at them in light of your vision.

Ask yourself whether they serve the character, the setting, the subject matter, the theme and/or the larger work. Ask yourself whether they propel your story forward. If they don't, delete them and file them for use in a future project.

Ask yourself whether they impede the story's pace and flow. If they do, delete them and file them for use in a future project.

Ask yourself how your work would be affected if you removed them? If nothing would change, delete them and file them for use in a future project.

¶ *Revisit Secret #6 in "12½ Secrets to Whole-Brain Editing."*

15. Write the Right word

The UPI stylebook includes a journalist's version of this apocryphal commandment: "A burro is an ass. A burrow is a hole in the ground. As a journalist you are expected to know the difference."

Part of the revision process involves ensuring (insuring?) that when it comes to these sometimes arcane distinctions, you write it right. Is it "affect" or "effect"? Is it "further" or "farther," "less" or "fewer," "passed" or "past"? When is it "then" and when is it "than"? How do you distinguish between these variants? Or ought you distinguish *among* them?

What follows is an alphabetical list of seventy-three ways those distinctions can sometimes screw you up. Unsure which is appropriate in your context? Look it up — in a dictionary, in a grammar/usage book or online.

1. aid / aide / AIDS
2. a lot / allot
3. aberrant / abhorrent
4. access / excess
5. accept / except
6. adverse / averse
7. advice / advise
8. affect / effect
9. all ready / already
10. allusion / elusion / illusion
11. all together / altogether
12. altar / alter
13. alternate / alternative
14. amicable / amiable
15. among / between
16. amoral / immoral
17. amount / number / quantity
18. any way / anyway / anyways / anyhow
19. any more / anymore
20. a part / apart
21. ascent / assent
22. assure / ensure / insure
23. aural / oral
24. breath / breathe
25. bring / take

26. burro / burrow
27. can / may / might
28. capital / capitol
29. cite / sight / site
30. complement / compliment
31. connect to / connect with
32. conscience / conscious
33. council / counsel
34. councilor / counselor
35. decent / descent / descant
36. elicit / illicit
37. e.g. / i.e
38. emigrate / immigrate
39. ensure / insure
40. eminent / immanent / imminent
41. every day / everyday
42. exalted / exulted
43. farther / further
44. fewer / less
45. figuratively / literally
46. flaunt / flout
47. good / well
48. I / me
49. imply / infer
50. in to / into
51. it's / its
52. lay / lie
53. lead / led
54. like / such as
55. loose / lose
56. passed / past
57. pray / prey
58. precede / proceed
59. principal / principle
60. right / rite / write
61. raise / rise
62. reluctant / reticent
63. sew / sow
64. stationary / stationery
65. suppose / supposed to
66. their / there / they're
67. than / then
68. that / which / who / whom
69. threw / through / thorough / though / thru
70. to / too / two
71. wait for / wait on
72. who's / whose
73. you're / your

16. Double-check Your Facts and Figures

Whether you're writing fiction, nonfiction (including memoir) or script, nothing ruins your credibility with readers more than factual errors. Of course, you're entitled to a degree of creative license when crafting a fictional account. At the same time, unless what you're writing is billed as "alternative reality," each time you stray from widely known facts, you jolt your readers enough to interrupt their flow and, perhaps, stop them from reading altogether.

If your story includes historical or celebrity names, statistics, recorded dates or geographical, biographical or other verifiable information, verify it. That's part of your job as editor. And if you are intentionally altering known facts in a book or short story, consider appending an "author's note" where you separate fact from fiction for your readers.

17. Curb Your Exclamations

A sure sign of amateur writing is the overuse of the exclamation mark!!! Let the content of your text or dialogue do the exclaiming, and don't rely on punctuation to make your point for you. As F. Scott Fitzgerald told Hollywood journalist Sheila Graham, "An exclamation point is like laughing at your own joke."

Don't laugh at your own jokes.

As you revise, use your application's find-and-replace function to ferret out all your exclamation marks, and consider replacing at least seventy-five percent of them with a commonplace period. You may be able to delete some outright; in other cases, you will have to rewrite the sentence for the desired effect.

18. Be Typographical

Adding two spaces after a period is a relic of typewriters and fixed-width fonts. With the proportional fonts used in today's publishing software, an extra space between sentences can disrupt the clean look of your text, especially when it's right-justified. Like before and after this sentence. Or like after this one. The extra space looks awkward and ought to be avoided unless you want your work to look amateurish.

Ninety-five percent of computer fonts are proportional (Courier, used in screenwriting, is the standout exception), and *no* professionally produced book is typeset with two spaces following a period. Unless there's a design reason for doing so, leave only a single space between sentences.

Easy fix: Conduct a find-and-replace search before you finalize your final draft. In most writing applications, type two spaces in the "find" field and one space in the "replace" field, then select "replace all." (Don't "replace all" if you have used extra spacing for other purposes; in a table or chart, for instance.)

While we're on the subject of typography, the professional standard is to use "smart" (curly) quotation marks and apostrophes (" ' "), not straight ones (' and "). The good news is that you should be able to set your device and/or app preferences to default to smart quotation marks and never have to think about it.

Well, almost never.

Certain apps do force you to think about it. In some, for example, direct typing on the keyboard defaults to smart quotes, but autocorrect and voice-to-text default to straight quotes.

Should your work end up with a scattering of straight quotation marks among the smart ones, be sure to curl all the offenders in one of your later drafts.

Finally, avoid using tabs or your space bar to indent. Instead, use your writing app's formatting function to set up the first line of your paragraphs, along with any other places where text must be indented. Tabs in writing apps rarely convert well when imported into publishing software.

19. Proofread

Computers are terrific. Mobile devices too. They make it easier than ever not only to write our books, poems, essays, short stories, stage plays and screenplays. They make it easier than ever to correct our mistakes.

I doubt there's a writing application out there that doesn't include a built-in dictionary and some form of spellcheck or autocorrect function. Increasing numbers also alert you to grammatical errors. On top of that, many screenwriting programs scan your script to ensure that your formatting conforms to industry standards.

In theory, that means that our scripts, manuscripts and published books are all error-free. Right?

Wrong.

Run your application's spellcheck and grammar-check functions. But don't rely on them to catch all typos and other errors.

Here's what your writing app gets right:

- *Speed:* It scans your script or manuscript for errors more quickly than you can.

- *Accuracy:* It easily flags and corrects your most blatant spelling errors, typos and grammatical faux pas.

- *Precision:* It catches easy-to-miss punctuation errors.

- *Batch Actions:* Its global find-and-replace function quickly corrects multiple instances of a single error and effects any draft-wide changes or standardizations you ask of it.

- *Time-Saving:* It frees you to focus the bulk of your editing efforts on content, style, context, etc.

Here's what your writing app can't do:

- *Homophones:* It can't distinguish between easily confused words like pray/prey, to/too/two, their/there/they're, etc.

- **Precision:** It can't catch any incorrectly used word if it's spelled correctly. Here's an example I found while proofreading this book. It's from "The Seven Elements of Authentic Dialogue" in Section 9...or it was until I corrected it: "Most of us don't stop in mid-speech to figure out whether 'who' or 'whom' is right or how to avoid ending our sentence with a proposition."
- **Context:** It can't relate words and sentences to what precedes or follows them, can't always distinguish between questions and statements and assumes all repeated words to be errors.
- **Missing Words:** It points them out only rarely, if at all.
- **Spacing:** It can't recognize extra or missing spaces.
- **Punctuation:** It can't flag missing or misplaced commas, nor can it handle the proper use of quotation marks in multi-paragraph speeches (see "Dialogue and Punctuation," Section 9).
- **Proper Nouns:** It may try to change names it can't recognize. Alternatively, it may ignore all capitalized words other than "I" and the first letter of a new sentence.
- **Content/Style/Consistency/Usage:** It can't cope with any of those. In other words, it can't...
- **Edit Like a Human!**

Here's how your writing app's correction tools can get in your way. They...

- **Distract:** Enabling spellcheck and grammar check while we're writing can impair our creative flow.
- **Make Us Less Observant:** We proofread less carefully (if at all) because we assume our writing app has caught all our mistakes.
- **Dull Our Critical Faculties:** It's easier to assume that the app knows what it's doing and to rely on its mechanistic fix than it is to think through a potential problem and come up with a creative solution.
- **Make Us Lazy:** We pay less attention to our spelling, punctuation and grammar — and become poorer spellers, punctuators and grammarians — because we assume our computer or its software will catch all our mistakes.

Here are some spellcheck and grammar check do's and don'ts:

- *Don't* run spellcheck and grammar check while you're writing.
- *Don't* use spellcheck and grammar check as a replacement for eagle-eyed proofreading and insightful editing.
- *Don't* accept all spellcheck and grammar check suggestions.
- *Do* vet all autocorrect, spellcheck and grammar check recommendations before accepting them.
- *Do* improve your grasp of spelling, punctuation, grammar.
- *Do* read your script or manuscript closely and with care.
- *Do* double-check all proper nouns, as well as anything your spellcheck and grammar check tools are not equipped to scrutinize.
- *Do* hire proofreaders and editors where appropriate. (See also "Next Steps," Section 14.)

In a 2005 UK survey, thirty-nine percent of respondents claimed to rely solely or mostly on their device's spellchecker. Unfortunately, a similar percentage could not identify the correct spelling of such words as "definitely," "separately" and "necessary."

Your application's built-in correction functions are valuable tools. Don't rely on them exclusively.

20. Be True to Your Vision

Every word you alter, every comma you add, every correction you make is for the sole purpose of shaping your story to be the best expression of your vision that your art, heart and skill can manage at this stage in your creative development and to communicate that vision as expertly as you are able. Let your vision statement keep you aligned with that vision and connected to it. Be true to your vision.

8. Slim, Trim and Simple

Let the reader find that he cannot afford to omit any line of your writing because you have omitted every word that he can spare.
RALPH WALDO EMERSON

Use the smallest word that does the job
E.B. WHITE

Thirty-Three Words and Phrases That Weaken Your Writing

The words and phrases on this list often serve no purpose. Where the meaning of your sentence won't be impaired, delete them. Where that isn't possible, see if you can rewrite your sentence for clarity or seek out replacement words or phrases that more imaginatively and originally express your vision and intent.

At the same time, remember Secret #1: There are no rules. Creativity is an art, and Ben Blatt's statistics in *Nabokov's Favorite Word Is Mauve* notwithstanding, writing can never be reduced to a catalog of absolutes and unbreakable commandments. Use your discernment.

Sometimes, for example, these "filler" words and phrases contribute to the rhythm, cadence and flow of a sentence, and that may be reason enough to retain them. In this book, I chose to keep the words "both" and "either" in a handful of instances where a sentence read better with them, even though the meaning was clear without them.

Once again, reading aloud — and *listening* — helps. Always.

very, really, quite, rather

These four modifiers nearly always weaken your writing. As adjectives or adverbs, they are rather/quite/very/really lazy replacement for more evocative language.

Kansas journalist William Allen White had a "very" good suggestion.

In a statement erroneously attributed to Mark Twain[1], White said, "Substitute 'damn' every time you're inclined to write 'very.' Your editor will delete it and the writing will be just as it should be."

Before: Jack drove very quickly to the store.
After: Jack raced to the store.

Before: Jill was really hungry.
After: Jill was ravenous.

Before: He was quite hot.
After: Rivulets of perspiration streamed down his face.

Before: "I really liked the concert."
After: "I liked the concert" / "The concert was better than I expected."

The preceding "after" examples could be more informative. How much did he like the concert? What did she like about it?

¶ *See also "Twenty-Five Damn Good Replacements for 'Very,'" next chapter.*

nice, interesting

These words are so vague as to say nothing. Revisit Revision Tip #8 and replace vagueness with specifics.

Before: Jill wore a nice dress.
After: Jill wore a vivid floral print.

Before: It was a nice day.
After: The late afternoon sun glinted off the mirrored glass of the Times Tower, casting its neighbors along the street in a golden glow. The air had cooled, although not enough for him to don the jacket slung over his shoulder. It was perfect shirtsleeves weather.

actually, basically, virtually

Actually, these words serve virtually no purpose and can basically be deleted.

---

[1] https://quoteinvestigator.com/tag/william-allen-white

Before: "We actually have soup on the menu."
After: "We have soup on the menu."

Before: "Basically, I want to go to college."
After: "I want to go to college."

just

In uses similar to those in the following examples, this is rarely a keeper.

Before: "I just want to know what you mean."
After: "Tell me what you mean."

Before: The mailbox was just around the corner.
After: The mailbox was around the corner.

literally

The primary dictionary definition of "literally" is "in a literal manner or sense; exactly." More often than not, however, it's used, as *Merriam-Webster* notes, "in an exaggerated way to emphasize a statement or description that is not literally true or possible."

"Literally" is rarely used correctly and rarely needed, unless in dialogue as part of a character's style of speech. Although as the example demonstrates, even in dialogue it can be superfluous.

Before: "That guitar solo literally blew my mind!"
After: "That guitar solo blew my mind!"

up, down

If most uses of "up" and "down" are justifiable, the following examples demonstrate that not all are.

Before: She climbed up the stairs.
After: She climbed the stairs.

Before: He sat down on the floor.
After: He sat on the floor.

begin to, start to

Watch for instances where these phrases serve no purpose. Where they are necessary to indicate the initiation of an action, find more powerful ways to express it.

Before: As the curtain came down, she started to cry.
After: As the curtain fell, she burst into tears / she could no longer hold back her tears / she sobbed noisily.

totally, completely

A descriptive adjective or verb renders these adverbs totally and completely redundant. The second example also converts a passive sentence into an active one. (See Revision Tip #4.)

Before: The drawer was totally/completely full.
After: The drawer was full. / The drawer was stuffed.

Before: The old theater was totally destroyed by fire.
After: Fire destroyed the old theater.

absolutely

An absolutely empty modifier.

Before: Ginger was sitting absolutely still.
After: Ginger sat motionless.

Before: Fred was absolutely certain.
After: Fred was certain. / Fred had no doubts.

that

Is your sentence clear without including "that"? Not sure? Read it aloud.

Before: It was the best photograph that she had ever shot.
After: It was the best photograph she had ever shot. / It was the most professional-looking photograph she had ever shot.

in order to

Nearly always unnecessary padding.

Before: She took the elevator to the fifth floor in order to buy herself a new dress.
After: She rode the elevator to the fifth floor to buy herself a new dress.

currently, at this point in time

The fact that something *is* nearly always places it in the present moment, which renders both terms unnecessary.

Before: Mary currently has a little lamb.
Before: At this time, Mary has a little lamb.
After: Mary has a little lamb.

see, hear

In the examples below, "see" and "hear" insinuate themselves between you and your reader. Unless context requires it, don't insulate yourself; be direct.

Before: "I could see him running toward me."
After: "He ran toward me." / "He sprinted toward me."

Before: "I could hear the radio blaring in the other room."
After: "The radio blared from the other room."

of, of the

Where they serve no useful purpose, delete them.

Before: He fell off of the chair.
After: He fell off the chair. / He tumbled from the chair.

Before: Hope lived inside of her.
After: Hope lived inside her.

Before: One of the executives at the cannery…
After: A cannery executive …

both, either

When content and context make it clear that two parties or objects are unequivocally involved, "both" can be redundant. Treat "either" similarly.

Before: Both Fred and Ginger saw the accident.
After: Fred and Ginger saw the accident. / Fred and Ginger witnessed the accident.

Before: "Either red or yellow. I don't care."
After: "Red or yellow. I don't care."

there is, there are

Often superfluous as sentence-openers.

Before: There are two police officers at the entrance.
After: Two police offers guard the entrance.

own

Frequently redundant. (I found the following example on one of my final read-throughs of this book.)

Before: Screenwriting is a collaborative endeavor. Producers have their own ideas. Directors have their own ideas. Actors have their own ideas.
After: Screenwriting is a collaborative endeavor. Producers have their ideas. Directors have their ideas. Actors have their ideas.

particular, specific

Delete when they add nothing to the sentence. (Here's another example I discovered on one of my final read-throughs.)

Before: Why did you write this particular story? What kind of impact do you hope it will have?
After: Why did you write this story? What kind of impact do you hope it will have?

Twenty-Five Damn Good Replacements for "very"

Can you substitute each "very" on this list with a single strong adjective? Turn the page for my list of potential replacements. (Although I have included only one suggestion for each, I'm sure you can come up with at least half a dozen.)

When editing your story, consult your friend the thesaurus (Revision Tip #2) to find the synonyms that best suit your context and intended meaning and eliminate as many instances of "very" as possible from your draft.

1. Very angry —
2. Very bad —
3. Very crowded —
4. Very different —
5. Very dumb —
6. Very fast —
7. Very full —
8. Very good —
9. Very noisy —
10. Very often —
11. Very old —
12. Very painful —
13. Very poor —
14. Very powerful —
15. Very pretty —
16. Very quiet —
17. Very rainy —
18. Very rich —
19. Very sad —
20. Very scared —
21. Very serious —
22. Very short —
23. Very shy —
24. Very smart —
25. Very unsure —

Twenty-Five Damn Good Replacements

1. Very angry — *enraged*
2. Very bad — *inferior*
3. Very crowded — *mobbed*
4. Very different — *distinctive*
5. Very dumb — *ignorant*
6. Very fast — *swiftly*
7. Very full — *stuffed*
8. Very good — *outstanding*
9. Very noisy — *booming*
10. Very often — *frequently*
11. Very old — *ancient*
12. Very painful — *excruciating*
13. Very poor — *impoverished*
14. Very powerful — *robust*
15. Very pretty — *stunning*
16. Very quiet — *hushed*
17. Very rainy — *teeming*
18. Very rich — *affluent*
19. Very sad — *dejected*
20. Very scared — *terror-struck*
21. Very serious — *dire*
22. Very short — *diminutive*
23. Very shy — *bashful*
24. Very smart — *savvy*
25. Very unsure — *hesitant*

Nabokov's Favorite Word Is Mauve. What's Yours?

All writers favor certain words and phrases. Nabokov's, according to Ben Blatt's calculations in *Nabokov's Favorite Word Is Mauve*, was, of course, "mauve." Isaac Asimov's was "terminus," Edith Wharton's was "compunction" and Virginia Woolf's was "mantelpiece." For Blatt to class them as favorites, those words had only to be used in half an author's books, at least once per hundred thousand words, and could not be proper nouns.

Although we don't necessarily overuse our favorites, all writers have particular words and phrases we unwittingly use to excess.

I have curbed my reliance on "very," but I still remain guilty of just too many justs, too many stills and even too many evens. I also start too many sentences with "once again" and, in my fiction, have my characters smile, laugh and nod with alarming frequency.

If I have edited effectively, you will find only limited evidence of those overindulgences in my published books. That's because, having identified at least some of the words and phrases I tend to lean on, I devote one later draft to conducting a global search for each and deleting or replacing as many as I can.

As you read and reread your work from draft to draft, do your best to become aware of the words and phrases you over-favor. Note them, and when you are approaching your final draft, go on a "favorites diet."

Keep It Simple...but Not Too Simple

Be simple. Be direct. Avoid jargon. Avoid four- or five-syllable words when words of one or two syllables tell the story as effectively. Avoid paragraph-long James Joycean sentences when a series of shorter ones would be clearer and easier to follow. Don't bury your reader in flowery excess. Don't show off.

In simplicity lies power and, as Leonardo da Vinci put, refinement: "Simplicity," he wrote, "is the ultimate sophistication."

At the same time, follow Albert Einstein's advice: "Everything should be made as simple as possible, but not simpler." In other words, don't oversimplify. Don't talk down to your readers. Use language that is audience- and age-appropriate, and remember Revision Tips #6 and 7: Don't overexplain and don't under-explain.

Trim the Fat

Have you used two or three words — or sentences — where one would do? Have you overwhelmed your reader with imagery or description that doesn't move your story forward, that doesn't reveal character, that strays from your central theme or idea? Have you unintentionally repeated scenes or descriptions? Have you needlessly reprised explanations, illustrations, examples or arguments or included variations that unnecessarily restate something you have already said?

Use all the tips in this section and Section 7 to keep your work lean and trim. Compress to say more with less.

This is particularly important in screenwriting, where concise writing is essential. But whether you are revising a sprawling epic, an encyclopedic work of nonfiction, a poem, a short story or a screenplay, your work would likely benefit from a gentle (or not-so-gentle) diet.

Compact writing that packs a punch isn't easy: "I have made this letter longer," Blaise Pascal wrote five centuries ago, "because I have not had the time to make it shorter." Take the time, and aim for lean, powerful writing.

In early drafts, of course, give yourself permission to free your writing to ramble at length. Use later drafts to trim the fat.

Try This

Get a Twitter account and practice writing posts of substance that don't exceed the social network's 280-character maximum. If you're more ambitious, limit your tweets to Twitter's previous 140-character limit.

Try This Too

Tighten these two plumped up excerpts as much as you can, without stripping them of interest and important information. Compare your versions with the originals at the end of the chapter.

"Sara's Year" novel (95 words)
Anne Savage couldn't help but notice the girl with the ponytail whose eyes were nearly as dark as her hair. It was easy for Anne to notice her. Most of the girls in her art classes were happy to be there, although she couldn't be sure whether it was because they loved the arts or because they were indifferent to their more academic subjects. But Esther Finkel? Esther was so very different. She had a spark…and a spark of talent. This girl would definitely amount to something. Anne Savage was absolutely certain of it.

"The MoonQuest" screenplay (57 words)
"Suns" is not a typo; in the world of this story, there are two suns in the sky.
Toshar wakes up. He is leaning back against the trunk of a broad, ancient tree, which sits at the center of a plateau that is, itself, suspended far above the suns and the clouds. The plateau is shaped like an irregular circle and is studded with colorful wildflowers. He sees no way back down to the ground.

Originals

"Sara's Year" novel (77 words)
Anne Savage noticed the ponytailed girl with eyes nearly as dark as her hair. She was easy to notice. Most of the girls in her art classes were enthusiastic, although whether it was for a love of the arts or an indifference to their academic subjects, she could never be sure. But Esther Finkel? Esther was different. She had a spark…and a spark of talent. This girl would amount to something. She was certain of it.

"The MoonQuest" screenplay (27 words)
Screenplay descriptions are necessarily compact, compressing as much information as possible into few words.
Toshar wakes under a broad, ancient tree in the center of an irregularly circular, flower-studded plateau far above suns and clouds. He sees no way down.

9. Refining Your Dialogue

Your readers don't want realistic speech, they want talk which spins the story along.
NIGEL WATTS

"And what is the use of a book," thought Alice, "without pictures or conversations?"
LEWIS CARROLL

Is Your Dialogue Doing Its Job?

If you have written fiction, memoir, script or any other form involving speech, make sure your dialogue strengthens your story, not weakens it.

Effective dialogue brings the people in your stories to life. It reveals character and reveals the relationships between characters. It can even reveal the relationship between a character and his or her environment.

Effective dialogue sets the scene, establishes mood, stirs up emotion and builds tension. Effective dialogue advances plot, foreshadows future events, recapitulates something significant from previous chapters and communicates backstory.

More often than not, it does it all obliquely and indirectly.

What effective dialogue doesn't do is feed your reader information that a character already knows, as in this example: "You know your brother Jack?" Ginger asked Fred. "The car thief?"

Fred knows who his brother is and, likely, knows he's a car thief. Dialogue like this always sounds forced and unnatural. If it's something you need the reader to know, find a way to relay it indirectly and avoid force-feeding large chunks of information through dialogue, simply because you don't know any other way to relate it.

Effective dialogue doesn't *tell* your readers something you can *show* them. Remember Revision Tip #5? Rework any "telling" dialogue in a way that *shows* readers what's important for them to know — through action, description and/or dialogue that's less direct. Make it natural to the character, to the situation. Don't have Jill tell Jack, "I'm sad." Show Jill being sad and show us why she's said. Have her say something like,

"I can't help thinking about Mom today. I can't believe I've lived longer without her in my life than I did with her."

As you revise your work, remove or rewrite any dialogue that isn't doing its job. And recognize that sometimes the best dialogue is no dialogue. Don't use dialogue as filler. Don't use dialogue where action or description is more dynamic. And don't use action or description when dialogue is better-suited to the task.

The Seven Elements of Authentic Dialogue

1. Authentic Dialogue Is Life*like*, Not *True*-Life

Authentic dialogue does not reproduce "real" speech. That's because real speech is nearly always fragmented, convoluted, rambling, awkward and incomplete. Real speech is peppered with clichés and ums and uhs. Real speech is filled with interruptions and irrelevancies. Authentic dialogue *sounds* real but isn't.

2. Authentic Dialogue *Can* Mimic Real Speech

Fictional speech, like yours and mine, isn't always grammatically correct. Most of us don't stop in mid-speech to figure out whether "who" or "whom" is right or how to avoid ending our sentence with a preposition. That's equally true of your characters.

We rarely address the person we're talking to by name. "You know, Jack, I think I'll apply for that job" reads as awkwardly on the page as it sounds when we hear it on the street.

We nearly always use contractions when we speak — "can't" instead of "cannot," "don't" instead of "do not," "isn't instead of "is not." Unless avoiding contractions is a particular character's speech pattern or he or she uses the non-contracted form for emphasis ("Do *not* take the car!"), contractions sound more natural.

3. Authentic Dialogue Is Compact and Concise

Real-life conversation isn't compact and concise. Real-*sounding* conversation is.

Distill each speech to its essence, removing anything superfluous.

Greetings and salutations, for example, are generally unnecessary. And scene-setup is best accomplished through action and exposition. Alfred Hitchcock once said that "drama is life with the dull bits cut out." The same holds true for dramatic dialogue. Enter the conversation as late in the scene as possible to avoid those "dull bits."

As well, avoid long unbroken monologues; trim them back to their essence or weave in action, description (including body language) or paraphrasing. Or insert another character's reactions or responses to convert monologue into dialogue.

Finally, keep sentences brief. Long, rambling sentences are difficult to follow in any context, particularly in dialogue. Unless they are in some way critical to the story, the character or the situation, avoid them.

4. Authentic Dialogue Is True-to-Character.

Authentic dialogue sounds like your characters not like you. Authentic dialogue is true to each character's rhythm, style, cadence and vocabulary and reflects that character's age, location, background, education, occupation, beliefs and tendencies.

Authentic dialogue expresses the unique way individual characters respond to different people and different situations. Authentic dialogue reveals each character's vision and intent, although not always directly. Authentic dialogue takes you into each character's heart and head.

Avoid putting words into your character's mouth. Instead, *listen* to your characters. Listen for their words and listen for their voice.

"In all of my writing," thriller writer Lawrence Block has written, "the most effective dialogue has been that which my characters supplied themselves; I've sat at the typewriter feeling rather like a courtroom stenographer, jotting down lines that other voices have shouted or whispered deep within my mind. I do my best work when I feel least like its source and most like its channel."

Just as you connected in an intuitive and visionary fashion with your work as whole, do the same with your characters. If you need help listening, adapt one of the "Talk to Your Story" meditations from Secret #7 and, instead, talk to your characters.

5. Authentic Dialogue Is Indirect

We rarely say precisely what we mean, and the same is true for your characters. Like the rest of us, they will often say the opposite of what they mean, deflect when asked a direct question and change the subject when they are uncomfortable or have something to hide.

Give your readers the space to read between the lines to interpret what your characters mean. Challenge them to notice what your character *isn't* saying.

This can be a powerful opportunity to include action and body language to reveal the truth behind the words.

6. Authentic Dialogue Is Impressionist

A little goes a long way when it comes to dialect, slang, clichés, profanity and heavy accents. Too much and your dialogue will be difficult for readers to follow. Include only a hint, enough to communicate the non-standard speech pattern but not so much that readers will stumble over it or struggle with it.

7. Authentic Dialogue Is Musical

Authentic dialogue is more than talk. It's music that helps set the mood, pace and rhythm of each scene and of the story as a whole. Revisit Revision Tip #10 and let *all* your language sing, including your dialogue.

He Said, She Said

Dialogue tags are the phrases that indicate to the reader who's saying what (he said/she said), and they are often superfluous. Why? Because context and content generally make it clear which character is speaking, and unnecessary tags inhibit the flow and pace of an exchange.

When tags are required, don't struggle for descriptive replacements for the standard he said/she said. He said/she said may seem boring and repetitive, but when not used to excess, it is nearly as invisible as words like "the" and "a." Highly visible and potentially distracting, however, are graphic verbs like "enthused," "shouted," "argued," "spat" and "yelped." Use them sparingly and judiciously.

And beware tags unrelated to speech: We don't "smile," "nod," "cough" or "shrug" our words. Where appropriate, though, we can smile, nod, cough or shrug mid-speech or before or after a line of speech.

In a screenplay, a "wryly" is a parenthetical dialogue direction that indicates the mood, tone or attitude the writer wants an actor to assume and it generally indicates amateurish screenwriting.

```
                    GINGER
                 (wryly)
         Hurry up. It's getting late. We need
         to get going.
```

The equivalent in prose is when you use an adverb to modify a dialogue tag: "He said smugly," "she said sadly," "he said laughingly," "she said smilingly." Avoid as many of these as you can, in both fiction and screenwriting, and rely instead on content and action to convey mood, tone and attitude.

Dialogue and Punctuation

What follows are standard North American practices for English-language texts. If you're working in a different language or another part of the world, familiarize yourself with relevant practices and follow them. (I adapted the first three series of examples from my novel *Sara's Year*.)

Seven Keys to Proper Dialogue Punctuation

1. Begin each speaker's speech on a new line with a new paragraph.

"Did your mother ever tell you about your name?" Sarah asked. She ran her fingers along the worn-leather spine of the book.

"Bernard was for my great grandfather, her grandfather."

2. Use quotation marks to enclose all speech.

"Then there was Harold." Bernie shuffled through the stack of books.

"Your mother sure knew how to pick them. All of them." Sarah chuckled. Her chuckle dissolved into a sigh. "Me too."

3. Place dialogue punctuation inside quotation marks.

Incorrect: "Your mother was the pretty one. Your mother was the smart one".
Correct: "Your mother was the pretty one. Your mother was the smart one."
Incorrect: "She did it to make me feel more like I belonged in Quebec"?
Correct: "She did it to make me feel more like I belonged in Quebec?"
Incorrect: "Bad news, girls", she said, gesturing toward a table by the window.
Correct: "Bad news, girls," she said, gesturing toward a table by the window.

4. Working with speech fragments, quoted text or the title of a song, poem or short story? Place all punctuation other than commas and periods *outside* the closing quotation mark (unless the punctuation is part of the original quotation).

Dickens opened *A Tale of Two Cities* with "it was the best of times, it was the worst of times."

Didn't Dickens open *A Tale of Two Cities* with "it was the best of times, it was the worst of times"?

"It was the best of times, it was the worst of times"; that's how Dickens opened *A Tale of Two Cities*.

Her favorite song is "Amazing Grace."
Is her favorite song "Amazing Grace"?
"Is your favorite song 'Amazing Grace'?"

The previous example is visually cumbersome, although it's technically correct. "Is 'Amazing Grace' your favorite song?" would be less awkward.

In this next series of examples, "Help!" (with exclamation mark) is the correct title of the song.

I love The Beatles' "Help!"
"Do you love The Beatles' 'Help!'?"

Another technically correct, but awkward-looking sentence. Less jarring would be something like this: "Do you love 'Help!' by The Beatles?"

5. Capitalize the first letter of the first word if the quotation is a complete sentence but not if it's a fragment.

He said, "Those soldiers are all cowboys."
He said the soldiers were "all cowboys."

"Go jump off a bridge," she said.
Did you just tell me to "go jump off a bridge"?

6. Use single quotation marks for text within a quoted speech that also takes quotation marks; the title of a short story, poem or song, for example, or speech within a speech.

"When they played 'The Star Spangled Banner,' not everyone stood."
"Do you know what he said? He said, 'When they played the national anthem, not everyone stood.'"

7. Is one speaker's speech longer than a single paragraph? Start each new paragraph with opening quotation marks, but use no closing quotation marks until the end of the speech's final paragraph.

This example from The StarQuest *also illustrates #6. (In this culture, storytelling uses a formal style of speech; hence, no contractions.)*

"At first, as a child, Àna would not be discouraged. She could not understand why such beautiful sounds were not allowed. She could not understand why it was forbidden to make such sounds when it felt so good to do so.

"'It is not about feeling good,' Àna's father scolded. 'It is about doing what is right.' He scowled, but only for a moment as scowls dull a star's twinkle. 'Singing is not right. So you will not do it.'"

Punctuation and Dialogue Tags

1. Does your speech end with a dialogue tag?

The verb is always lower case, regardless of any punctuation that precedes it.

"This is my speech," said Jack.
"Is this my speech?" asked Jack.
"This is my speech!" exclaimed Jack.

2. Inserting a dialogue tag mid-speech?

The second part of the speech starts a new sentence if the dialogue tag ends with period but not if it ends with a comma.

"This is my speech," said Jill. "That one's yours."
"This," said Jill, "is my speech."

3. Inserting action or description mid-speech?

In this example from Sara's Year, *each element is its own sentence and begins, as all sentences do, with an upper-case letter. Inserting action or description, as I have done here, performs double duty: It eliminates the need for a dialogue tag and illuminates the speech.*

"Only one scoop." Sarah patted her ample stomach. "I have to watch my figure."

10. Openings and closings

An opening line should invite the reader to begin the story. It should say: Listen. Come in here. You want to know about this.
STEPHEN KING

Your first chapter sells your book. Your last chapter sells your next book.
MICKEY SPILLANE

Seduce Your Readers

One of the best-known opening sentences of all time is also considered the worst. "It was a dark and stormy night," from Edward Bulwer-Lytton's 1830 novel *Paul Clifford*, which has been parodied more than perhaps any other line in publishing history. If you're a *Peanuts* fan, you'll recall that most of Snoopy's literary efforts began that way.

Those seven words, however, make up only a tiny slice of Bulwer-Lytton's fifty-eight-word behemoth, which goes like this: "It was a dark and stormy night; the rain fell in torrents — except at occasional intervals, when it was checked by a violent gust of wind which swept up the streets (for it is in London that our scene lies), rattling along the housetops, and fiercely agitating the scanty flame of the lamps that struggled against the darkness."

Perhaps that sentence seduced Bulwer-Lytton's nineteenth-century readers. It would do little for today's, other than as a kitschy entry in San José State University's annual Bulwer-Lytton Fiction Contest, which, since 1982, has sought out the most "atrocious opening sentence to a hypothetical bad novel."[1]

Your opening sentence is the most important one in your work, whatever your form, medium or genre. With it, you will hook your readers or lose them. Now is the time to make certain that your story has the strongest opening you can give it.

As you revise your work, ask yourself whether your first sentence has the power to accomplish these four key tasks:

1. Grab a reader's attention. In a bookstore, your book has eight seconds to hook a potential reader. Along with your front and back covers, your

---

[1] https://www.bulwer-lytton.com, "where 'www' means 'wretched writers welcome.'"

opening sentence is part of that eight-second sales pitch. Don't waste it.

2. *Draw readers swiftly into your world.* Whether your world is fictional or "real-life," your opening sentence is a gateway into that realm.

3. *Create a visceral bridge between you and your readers.* Without that emotional bond, however unconscious, readers are less likely to commit to your book. Your opening sentence is your first step in forging it.

4. *Entice readers into continuing.* Your opening sentence is like that first taste of a new or exotic dish. If it doesn't leave readers hungering for more, they will look elsewhere for their literary sustenance.

Querying an agent or a publisher? There's a fifth task, if don't want your work to get lost amidst the hundreds of scripts and manuscripts that cross agents' and publishers' desks every week. If your opening sentence doesn't grab them, they are unlikely to read past it. (That's true of your story, of course, but it's also true of your query letter.)

Novelist Kathryn Kuitenbrouwer reminds us that "a first line should hold the spark of tone that…will hopefully entrance the reader into the magic of the book."

Make *all* your sentences count, of course, but pay special attention to your opening and closing as your finalize your work. And speaking of closings…

About Your Ending

Your story's ending is nearly as important as its beginning. You don't want your readers to feel disappointed or cheated when they turn the last page. If they do, they are unlikely to recommend your writing or read anything else of yours.

There's nothing worse than having invested weeks or months in a book, only to reach the final chapter, scene, paragraph or sentence and regret your time spent with it. Don't leave your readers with that feeling.

Think about the closing bars of a symphony. Is your ending as satisfying as that? Or does it fall flat in some way?

Think of a fine wine and how the flavor and bouquet linger satisfyingly after you take a sip and swallow. You want your last sentence to linger with your readers in the same way. Does it?

When we finish a great story, we experience a mix of closure and continued connection, along with an eagerness to seek out more by the same writer. Does your work do that?

"A great last line," says sci-fi author David Gerrold, "should leave your reader satisfied that you have said everything that needs to be said — and at the same time, it should stand as a launchpad for the reader's imagination to leap off into its own flight of fantasy about what happens next."

This may be your last chance to fix a flawed ending. Do it!

11. The "Heartful Revision" Mindset

Creativity takes courage.
HENRI MATISSE

It is good to have an end to journey toward, but
it is the journey that matters in the end.
URSULA K. LE GUIN

celebrate!

I don't know whether it's human nature to focus on what we haven't accomplished and to ignore or belittle our achievements, or whether we have been educated and socialized to do it. Regardless, we spend much more time paying attention to our perceived mistakes, missteps and failures than we do acknowledging our successes.

That practice is not only counterintuitive, it's counterproductive. That's because, as the maxim goes, "energy flows where attention goes." In other words, the more we focus on our success, the more success we attract into our life.

If you're reading *The Heartful Art of Revision*, chances are you have completed a first draft of your story or are getting close. That, itself, is a singular accomplishment. Most people with creative ambitions rarely start a project, let alone make it as far as you have. That's a success worth acknowledging and celebrating.

So here's the first thing I want you to do before you start work on your second draft: Recognize the triumph that is your first draft...and celebrate it. Celebrate you.

When I was a kid in grade school, we got stickers and gold stars when we did well. Why? Because acknowledgments like those fired us up to do better. Incentives work. Meaningful incentives work.

What will your gold star be? What's your equivalent of the schoolroom sticker? How can you celebrate your achievement? How can you reward your success? What extra-special something can you do for yourself that validates your accomplishment? Maybe you can go away for the weekend. Or take yourself out to dinner. Or treat yourself to a massage. Or indulge in a gooey dessert or premium coffee drink. Or buy yourself a book you have always wanted. How about all of the above?

Don't limit your celebration to your first draft. Honor the completion of every new draft with a gold star. It doesn't have to be an expensive or extravagant indulgence. But whatever your reward, let it be something significant. You earned it, so celebrate!

Revisit Your Vision, Revisit Your Work

Before you begin your first revision and before you start every new draft, reread your vision statement — aloud, if possible. The sound of your voice will add power and resonance to your intent. Don't merely read it. Connect with it and, through it, connect with your work.

Hold this vision in your heart through each draft and each revision. Hold this vision when you send the final version out into the world. Hold this vision when you receive feedback or criticism. This vision will always keep you centered and aligned with the essence of your work.

Once you have revisited your vision, it's time to revisit your story.

Let Judgment Go

It isn't always easy to release our natural tendency toward self-criticism and self-censorship. Yet, the only way to polish and shape your work into the masterpiece that best expresses your vision for it is to release all judgment about it.

Before you read your first draft or any draft, ask yourself these questions:

- Am I ready to read my words from an openhearted place of non-judgment? Of objective discernment?
- Am I ready to partner with my story rather than control it? Do I feel able to surrender to its wisdom?
- Can I give myself permission to read from a place of consideration and compassion — for the story and for myself? From a place of trust in my innate creativity? From a place of trust in my Muse? In the heart of the story itself?
- If this is my first time going over my first draft, can I give myself permission to read it at least one time through without changing anything?

Unless you can answer yes, unequivocally, to all these questions, let your work sit unread until you can. Unless you can answer yes, you risk damaging your creation and your creativity by launching into editing too hastily. Unless you can answer yes, it is premature to do anything with what you have written other than set it aside for a time.

When you can honestly answer yes, remember Secret #6 and read with respect — for your work and for yourself.

If you need help settling into a space of non-judgment, set five to ten minutes aside for the meditation that follows in the next chapter, "The Spirit of Heartful Revision."

The Spirit of Heartful Revision

A Guided Meditation

Have your script or manuscript handy and move directly into editing from the meditation.

Allow 5-10 minutes for the experience.

A professionally recorded meditation similar to this one is available for download or streaming as part "The Voice of the Muse Companion: Guided Meditations for Writers." See "Guided Meditations" in Section 1 to find out how to access the recording, as well as for tips on how best to use this book's meditations.

Note that the recorded version, titled "Let Judgment Go," is longer than this one and focuses more on avoiding judgment as you write than as you edit.

Breathe. Breathe in the quiet, white light of your creative essence, your divine essence, your Muse. Breathe in your fire, your flame, your beingness, your intuitive self, your God-self. Breathe in the light of who you are, the truth of who you are, the love of who you are. Breathe in all the light and aloha you are.

Aloha is not merely a word that conjures up the gentle swaying of palm trees and hula dancers. Aloha is a consciousness, a state of being, a state of openheartedness, a state of love in its truest, fullest sense.

Breathe into that openness within you. That love within you. Breathe it in fully, deeply, completely.

Breathe out any doubts, any fears that you're not good enough, that someone else or anyone else — your friend who has already been published, your neighbor who writes better dialogue or description than you do — is a more accomplished creator.

Breathe that out, for it is not true.

Breathe that out, for it is not relevant.

Comparisons are never relevant.

Let go all feelings that you're not good enough. You are.

Release all feelings that others are better than you are. They are not.

Put aside all feelings that others could have written your story more compellingly than you did. They could not have.

You are equal to all and equal to the joyful task at hand, which is shaping the words and passions of your heart into the clearest, truest expression of your vision.

Not from a place of self-judgment. Not from a place of "less than." Not from a place of "not good enough."

From a place of humility and self-empowerment. From a place of self-respect and self-worth. From a place of celebration.

As you now prepare to read what you have written, as you ready yourself to move into and through a new draft of your work, breathe out judgment and breathe in discernment.

Breathe out blind criticism and breathe in perceptiveness.

Breathe out harsh self-talk and breathe in compassion.

Breathe out insecurity and negativity, and breathe in optimism, hope and heartfulness.

Breathe out comparisons with other writers and with other writing, and breathe in the light and essence of your vision.

Breathe out censorship and second-guessing, and breathe in the unique expression of your heart's vision.

Breathe out your mind's perceived need to control, and breathe in mindful surrender to the essence of your work, to the higher wisdom of your work.

Repeat aloud after me:

> *I [your name] surrender to my highest vision for ["my writing" or "your title, if you know it"], to its highest vision for itself and to its highest vision for me.*
>
> *As I read, reread, edit, rewrite and revise ["my work" or "your title"], I do so with without fear and without judgment, making*

only those alterations that will enhance the story and stories I am telling.

I now stand ready to shape my work into the masterpiece it deserves to be and that I deserve it to be.

And so it is.

Take another deep breath in as you anchor within you the statement you have affirmed. Breathe into your commitment. Breathe into your heart. Breathe into your work. Take another deep breath, in and out, and now another.

And when you feel ready to approach your work with an open mind, discerning eye, and generous heart, open your eyes and reach for it to begin a new round of revisions.

Pick it up, open to the first page or to wherever you left off and read it without judgment. Read it with respect for it. Read it with respect for yourself as its creator.

As you read it, let a keen eye and an open heart guide you, and let the deepest, innermost knowingness of your intuition pilot you through not only this draft but every draft...all the way through to the moment when you hold your writing project in its final form in your hands.

And now...begin.

12. Working with Your Drafts

> In any art...one of the deepest secrets of excellence
> is discernment.
> REX STOUT

> Grammar is a piano I play by ear, since I seem to have been out of school the year the rules were mentioned. All I know about grammar is its infinite power.
> JOAN DIDION

General Preparation

The best practice when editing your script or manuscript is to begin with a global overview. From there, let each successive draft consist of a more detailed revision, with your final drafts returning you to that "macro" view.

Here are six general tips to apply to every draft and revision:

1. Create a new document for each draft. It's easy, during revision, to make changes in one draft that you regret in the next. Working on a fresh (not overwritten) document is an easy and effective way to reevaluate your edits and alter or reverse them where necessary.

2. If possible, edit from a hard copy. You are more objective when you edit in a medium that's different from the one you wrote in; you are also more likely to catch problems you might otherwise miss. As well, having all your changes visible provides a handy "edit trail" that makes it easier to restore changes you later determine to have been unwise or premature. Working with a hard copy also helps with Tip #3.

3. For a fresh perspective on a particular draft, edit away from your normal work area and/or computer screen.

4. Can't resist making onscreen changes? Keep the original text visible by enclosing your change in square brackets, by underlining it or by displaying it in a different font or color.

5. Familiarize yourself with "version history," a feature that's part of MS Word, Apple's Pages, Final Draft and many other writing apps, sometimes under different names like "browse versions," "backup history" or "browse backups." It allows you to

access previous versions of your file. (Generally, the versions are saved automatically. Some apps require you to back up versions manually. In some apps, it's a preference you must enable.)

6. Use a backup system that saves not only the current version of your document to an external drive or off-site service, but previous versions as well. This not only insures you against lost or corrupted files, it allows you to access earlier drafts where necessary.

First Read-Through

1. ***Preparation I:*** Print your work, single-spaced with minimal margins. You will be making few if any notes, and reading from a printout like this (preferably, with no pen or pencil in hand) will help you avoid making changes. Alternatively, read from a PDF. If you must make notes, do no more than make light margin notes or PDF comments.

2. ***Preparation II:*** Reread your vision statement. Aloud.

3. ***Take a Global Overview:*** Read your first draft all the way through, aloud where practical, holding your vision in your heart and leaving aside doubt and self-criticism. Revisit "The Spirit of Heartful Revision" and "Let Judgment Go" in Section II should you need help.

4. ***Read in the Flow:*** Read for spirit, for a sense of the whole. If you wrote your first draft on the Muse Stream, read it from that same surrendered, free-flow place. This is a right-brain macro view, not a left-brain micro view. Read without judgment. Read for fun. This is your first opportunity to experience your full first draft, so...

5. ***Make No Changes:*** Resist the temptation to make major changes. Resist the temptation to make any changes. This read-through is not about close editing or detailed corrections.

First Read-Through Impressions

Now that you have experienced the "wholeness" of your first draft for the first time...

1. ***What Did You Think?*** Be objective — discerning, not judgmental. Revisit Secret #4, "Suspend Judgment."

2. ***Be Positive:*** Focus not only on what you got "wrong" but on what you got "right." Celebrate your work's strengths as well as being honest about its weaknesses. (Being honest doesn't mean "brutally" honest. Remember Secret #6: Respect All Your Drafts. And respect yourself.)
3. ***Be General:*** Note any other general impressions from this global overview.
4. ***Be Specific:*** What did you like, specifically, about your first draft? Did you notice any particular problems?
5. ***Make Notes:*** Now you can make notes. What will you want to remember when you launch into your next read-through?

Second Read-Through

Continue to resist the temptation to make substantive changes.

1. ***Preparation I:*** Reprint your draft, double- or triple-spaced this time, with generous margins. You'll be making notes and you want them to be clear and legible. If it isn't possible to work from a hard copy, work with your draft on your computer, using your writing app's in-document comments/notes feature or the notes feature of your PDF reader. (Although you will be making extensive notes on this read-through, you won't be making in-text changes.)

2. ***Preparation II:*** Revisit any notes and impressions from your first read-through. What strengths did you notice? What weaknesses? What would it be helpful to keep in mind on this new read-through?

3. ***Read with Your Whole Brain:*** After your "impressionist" first read-through, it is now time to read your draft more closely. Start to call in the critical and analytical skills of your left brain without neglecting the holistic skills of your right brain. Even as you note specifics (micro view), be sure to retain your awareness of the whole (macro view) and of patterns and connections. Again, suspend judgment and embrace discernment.

4. ***Make Notes:*** Make general notes in the margins and/or between the lines about things that need changing or that require closer scrutiny. Don't seek out potential/necessary edits; simply jot down any you happen to notice. These could include but are not limited to...
   - clichés, jargon and inappropriate words or images
   - superfluous or missing words
   - problem sentences, dialogue, description

- ambiguities, redundancies, inconsistencies, unintended meanings
- places where you have or under- or overexplained
- places where your characters are not acting/speaking credibly
- places where your story/narrative/argument is not clear or doesn't make sense
- places where something impedes the flow or simply feels "off"

Subsequent Read-Throughs

It is on these subsequent read-throughs that you will start making substantive changes to your document — those you have already noted, those covered in Sections 6, 7, 8, 9 and 10 of this book and any others that feel relevant. Avoid trying to deal with all ten categories outlined in the next chapter on the same read-through. Rather, consider a separate draft for each major category.

Depending on your story, you may be able to combine some categories into a single draft; others may require multiple drafts. As well, you may find it easier to deal with particular questions from one category as part of another. There are no rules.

However you proceed, don't neglect your intuition, remember to focus on discernment not judgment and continue to hold your vision in your heart as you align your work with its highest expression.

Don't forget to reread your vision statement before starting each new draft. How many drafts? As many as it takes.

Preparation

1. Was there anything from earlier read-throughs that demands immediate attention? Anything that it is important for you to keep in mind as you launch into each new draft?
2. Don't forget to read your vision statement before working on your story.
3. Don't forget to suspend judgment and embrace discernment. Again, if you need help, revisit "The Spirit of Heartful Revision" and "Let Judgment Go" (Section 11).
4. Don't forget to create a new document for each draft.

Your Ten-Step Revision Checklist

As you move through each draft, always ask how your writing can be clearer and more concise, dynamic and evocative and how your vision can be best expressed. Read aloud for clearer answers to many of these questions, especially those related to language and dialogue.

1. Passion & Vision

- ✓ Have you communicated your passion for your story or topic?
- ✓ Are your vision and intent clear? Does the story align with your vision?

2. Logic & Flow

- ✓ Does your narrative/story make sense?
- ✓ Does your narrative/story flow logically as written?
- ✓ Does any content (sentences/paragraphs/scenes/chapters/sections) need to be moved around to improve the flow/sense?
- ✓ Does any content not make sense in the context of the whole work?
- ✓ Are there gaps that leave out critical information/details/descriptions/instructions that will baffle or confuse your readers?

3. Openings & Closings

- ✓ Does your opening sentence seduce your readers? Is it engaging? Intriguing? Compelling? Does it drop your readers into a pivotal moment in your story?

- ✓ Do your opening scenes/chapters keep the pages turning?
- ✓ Does your closing scene bring your story to a satisfying conclusion? Does it offer a sense of completion and continued connection?
- ✓ Does your closing leave your readers eager for your next story?

4. General Content

- ✓ What have you under-explained? Overexplained?
- ✓ Have you given examples to help explain your ideas/concepts? Have you given too many examples? Are there clearer, more illustrative examples you could use?
- ✓ Are there inconsistencies you can clear up? Redundancies you can eliminate? Ambiguities you can clarify?
- ✓ Are there favorite sentences/descriptions/scenes/examples that fail to support the story or your vision? That fail to support your topic or theme?
- ✓ Are there favorite characters that serve no purpose in the story?
- ✓ Does anything else feel "off"?

5. Language

- ✓ Where are you "telling" instead of "showing"?
- ✓ Where can you replace passive sentences with active ones?
- ✓ Where can you evoke mystery and the unknown by replacing active sentences with passive ones?
- ✓ Where can you be more detailed in your descriptions? Where are you too detailed?
- ✓ Where can you use more imagery? Where can you link the images in your word pictures?
- ✓ Do all your sentences sound the same? Same length? Same style/structure?
- ✓ Does the type/length/style of your sentences support the scene you are trying to set and the mood you are seeking to evoke?

- ✓ Is your language and sentence-length appropriate for your genre/age/audience?
- ✓ Where can your language be clearer and more concise, vibrant and expressive?
- ✓ Where can you break free of your adjective/adverb crutches? Where can you replace weak adjectives, adverbs, nouns and verbs with more dynamic ones?
- ✓ Where can you replace clichés and jargon with original writing that provokes, astounds and astonishes?
- ✓ Where have you overused slang, dialect or expletives?
- ✓ Where have you used an incorrect, misleading or ambiguous word?
- ✓ Revisit "Thirty-Three Words and Phrases that Weaken Your Writing" and determine which you can remove or replace.
- ✓ Do you have a word or phrase you tend to overuse? Now is the time to go on a "favorites diet."

6. Dialogue

- ✓ Where is your dialogue not doing its job? Where is it acting as filler and not serving your story?
- ✓ Does your dialogue express your characters' vision and intent?
- ✓ Does your dialogue reflect your characters' age, location, background, education, occupation, beliefs and tendencies?
- ✓ Listen for rhythm and cadence. Does your dialogue sound natural or forced?
- ✓ Where does your dialogue not sound like "real people"?
- ✓ Where does your dialogue sound too much like real people? (Remember: Don't mimic real-life; sound true-to-life.)
- ✓ Where do different characters sound too much alike?
- ✓ Where does your dialogue sound more like your voice than your characters'?
- ✓ Where is your dialogue too direct? Where would it be better to

have your character say something other than what she or he thinks, knows or believes?
- ✓ Where is your dialogue bloated? Superfluous? Bland?
- ✓ Where does a speech run too long? Where can an overlong speech be trimmed, interspersed with action or description or converted into back-and-forth dialogue?
- ✓ Where are your characters explaining things best left to narration? Where can narration be better expressed as dialogue?
- ✓ Where are you using dialogue to feed readers information that would be best delivered in other ways? To feed readers information that the characters speaking it already know?
- ✓ Where have you used direct address in a way that sounds unnatural?
- ✓ Where have you failed to start a new paragraph every time a new person is speaking?
- ✓ Where is it not clear which character is speaking?
- ✓ Where have you over-tagged your dialogue?
- ✓ Where can you replace a "wryly" with clearer dialogue, description and/or action to more effectively convey mood, tone and attitude.

7. Structure

- ✓ Do your chapters/sections and other breaks make sense for the type/genre of your work?
- ✓ In your type of work, should chapter/section breaks complete a thought or theme? Or would they be better structured to build suspense?
- ✓ Are your chapters/sections and other breaks appropriate for the audience/reading level of your work?
- ✓ Do your chapter/section breaks seem natural? Forced?
- ✓ Are some paragraphs are too long? Too short?
- ✓ Are some chapters too long or too short? Short chapters build suspense and keep the pages turning. Lengthy chapters are more

contemplative. Chapters that are too long, however, can appear daunting. Are there chapters that might work better in shorter chunks? Too-brief chapters that ought to be merged?

✓ Can you be more creative with the chapter/section breaks in your nonfiction in ways that support better engagement?

✓ Can you present the information in your nonfiction in ways that will render it more visually appealing? For example, can you replace some paragraphs with bulleted or numbered lists? Can you break up chapters with subheadings?

8. Spelling, Punctuation & Grammar

✓ Have you run your application's spellcheck and grammar check?

✓ Have you checked manually for the spelling/punctuation/grammar errors your application is ill-suited to flag and correct?

✓ Have you double-checked the spelling/consistency of all proper nouns, including people's/character names, pet/animal names, place names, brand names and historical events? Is your use of capitalization consistent?

✓ Have you double-checked the spelling/consistency of all foreign words and phrases and all made-up words? Is your use of capitalization correct and consistent?

✓ Have you double-checked all verifiable facts, including statistics, dates and biographical data, against reliable sources?

✓ Have you double-checked all quotes against reliable sources? The internet is awash with wrongly attributed quotations. Do your best to ensure their accuracy by finding primary sources. Sites like Quote Investigator (https://quoteinvestigator.com) and Wikiquote (https://en.wikiquote.org/wiki) can help.

✓ Where can you cut back on exclamation marks?

✓ Is your use of hyphenation consistent?

✓ Do you have too many commas? Too few? Let clarity be your guide.

✓ Do all your sentences begin with a capital letter?

- ✓ Do all your sentences end with a period and a single space? Professional typography does not end a sentence with two spaces.
- ✓ Have you removed all extra/unnecessary spaces between words?
- ✓ Is your dialogue punctuation correct and consistent?
- ✓ Are you missing any opening/closing quotation marks?
- ✓ Are all your quotation marks and apostrophes "smart" (curly)? Straight apostrophes/quotation marks (' and ") are rarely used in professional typography.

9. Style

- ✓ Do you mix American/British/Canadian spellings/styles?
- ✓ Is your use of italics for foreign words consistent?
- ✓ Is your use of quotation marks consistent (i.e. double v. single quotation marks)?
- ✓ Is your use of commas as consistent as you can make it? If you prefer Oxford/serial commas, do you use them throughout?
- ✓ Is your use of capitalization consistent?
- ✓ Is your use of numbers consistent? Individual style guides offer differing guidelines as to when to spell out a number. Choose your style and stick with it.
- ✓ Does your use of fonts, point sizes and spacing contribute to your final draft's readability?
- ✓ Is your use of fonts, point sizes and spacing consistent?

10. Format

- ✓ If you're submitting your work to an agent or publisher, does it meet all submission requirements?
- ✓ If you're self-publishing, is your formatting appropriate and consistent?
- ✓ If you have written a screenplay, does it meet industry formatting standards?

Almost-Final Read-Through

We launched the revision process with a general overview of your work. That was your first draft. From there, we moved to increasingly detailed edits of your subsequent drafts. It's now time to come full circle and revisit and revise your work from a global perspective.

Global Overview

1. Revisit your vision statement.
2. Read for the spirit of the work, for a sense of the whole.
3. Read with an open heart and mind.
4. Read aloud, where possible.
5. Review the tips and questions in the "First Read-Through" and "Second Read-Through" chapters.

Ask Yourself These Questions…and Be Honest

- ✓ Does the opening draw me in?
- ✓ Does the finished work still reflect my vision?
- ✓ Does my narrative/story make sense? Flow logically? Are there any scenes or chapters where something gets in the way of that flow, where something could cause a reader to stumble or struggle?
- ✓ Is the closing satisfying, while leaving me keen for more?
- ✓ Are there any remaining redundancies, inconsistencies, ambiguities?

- ✓ Are there any remaining story/information gaps?
- ✓ Are there any "favorites" that I haven't had the heart to eliminate?
- ✓ Is there anything that feels awkward, that I trip over while reading?
- ✓ Are there any changes I regret having made?
- ✓ Is there anything else that is conspicuously problematic?

Step Into Your Reader's Shoes

It is now time to take off your author's hat and read your work as though for the first time, as though you're a reader. As with all your drafts, take some time away from your script or manuscript before launching into this new read-through.

Ask yourself many of the same questions that you asked during your first, second and final read-throughs — but as a reader. If you need help being objective and it's a book you have written, flow your manuscript into a simple book-design template and print it out, or save it as a PDF. If it's a script, read a hard copy or PDF.

Ask Yourself These Questions...and Be Honest

- ✓ Does the title draw me in?
- ✓ Does the first sentence or scene draw me in?
- ✓ Does the work evoke the desired emotions? Do I laugh/cry in all the places as the reader that I did as the writer?
- ✓ Am I engaged? Is it a page-turner?
- ✓ Does the work spark a genre-appropriate response? Amusement? Curiosity? Hope? Suspense? Mystery? Engagement? Inspiration? Motivation? Enlightenment?
- ✓ Does the work come to a satisfying conclusion? Does the closing scene or sentence leave me feeling in some way fulfilled? Does it stay with me for a time after I finish? If I were a stranger, would the ending motivate me to seek out more from the writer?

Once More...with Feeling

If time permits, set the work aside for a week or a month or longer, then read it one final time with fresh eyes. Read it again from a global perspective. At the same time, watch for any nitpicky details you might have missed.

This could be your final read-through before submission or publication. Make it count.

13. The Screenwriter's Edit Suite

> You have to stay true to the voice, to what it is that distinguishes you as a writer.
> DAVID BRIND, SCREENWRITER

> I don't think that there's such a thing as a perfect script.
> DAVID S. WARD, OSCAR-WINNING WRITER OF *THE STING*

Much of what I cover in previous sections applies equally to screenwriting or can be adapted to screenplay revision. What follows are additional tips and a supplementary checklist particularly suited to editing your film script. Some of these can also be adapted to prose.

Six Revision Tips for Screenwriters

1. Evocative Language Matters

A screenplay is more than a mechanical how-to for director, actors and designers. Perhaps a more apt metaphor would be an artist's rendering, with its shapes and shadings, its eloquence and flair.

Just because the screenplay form demands brief sentences and paragraphs doesn't mean your script is not a literary work...is not a literary work designed to be read. Before it is ever viewed on a cinema screen, your script's first audience is always going to be an audience of readers. Seduce those readers with evocative writing that lets them *see* your movie on the pages of your screenplay. That's the first step toward getting a green light for development and production.

2. Compress, Compress, Compress

If evocative writing matters, so does concise writing — more in screenwriting than in any other literary form. Unlike a novelist, a screenwriter doesn't have the space to allow a single description to spill lyrically into multiple paragraphs. Even a short-story writer has more freedom in this regard than you do. Be powerful but spare in your use of language. As Thomas Jefferson put it: "The most valuable of all talents is that of never using two words when one will do."

3. Talk to Your Characters

Your screenplay is your characters' story, so trust them to know it better than you do. Talk to your characters. Let them tell you how their story needs to be told. Let them tell you what's not right about their story as you have written it. Let them tell you what's missing and what's superfluous. Let them guide you.

Listen to what your characters say and how they say it. Listen for their voice, their vocabulary, their inflection. Adapt one of the "Talk to Your Story" meditations from Secret #7 if you need help.

Remember what Lawrence Block said in "The Seven Elements of Authentic Dialogue" (Section 9): "In all of my writing, the most effective dialogue has been that which my characters supplied themselves."

Let *your* characters supply it.

4. Trust Your Audience

What have you overexplained? Today's filmgoers are considerably more sophisticated than they were in decades past. Trust your audience to be able to follow your story without being spoon-fed.

5. Trust Your Collaborators

Don't direct or design the film from the pages of your script: Remove all camera direction and delete all extraneous stage direction and design detail.

Delete anything that gets in the way of an actor's interpretation, including wrylies. The only exception would be where a line of dialogue could be interpreted multiple ways; where possible or appropriate in those situations, rewrite the line for clarity.

Retain enough detail and description to allow your director, production designer, cinematographer, locations manager, casting director and actors to communicate your vision. Remove anything that limits their imagination or cripples their ability to marry their vision to yours.

6. Empower Yourself

Recognize that filmmaking is a collaborative endeavor. Producers have their ideas. Directors have their ideas. Actors have their ideas. Unless you're producing, directing and acting in the film yourself, your final draft is unlikely to be *the* final draft. Scripts get changed.

Be open to suggestions. Be open to improvements. Get your ego out of the way and use your discernment to know when to fight, when to negotiate, when to hold your ground and when to give in. Don't compromise your integrity, but be flexible.

Empower yourself.

Your Twelve-Step Revision Checklist

1. Revisit your vision statement. Does your screenplay align with it?
2. Does your film come alive on the pages of your script?
3. Are your action paragraphs concise and evocative? Try to keep your action paragraphs to no more than four lines apiece.
4. Is your dialogue compelling? Does it move your story forward? Have you used dialogue where action might be more expressive?
5. Have you eliminated endless paragraphs of dialogue not broken up by action paragraphs and endless paragraphs of action unbroken by dialogue?
6. Are your characters convincing? Is their journey (character arc) credible? Compelling?
7. Does each scene build on the last, does each scene move the story forward and do all your scenes come together to create an engrossing story that builds to a riveting climax and satisfying conclusion?
8. Are your character and location descriptions specific enough to express your vision and meet the needs of your story but not so specific that they could hamstring the film's casting director and locations manager?
9. Have you stripped everything from your script that tells actors how to act, directors how to direct, cinematographers how to shoot and anyone else how to do their job? In other words, have you removed all camera direction, stage direction, actor direction and art direction?

10. Is your screenplay no longer than 120 pages (for a feature film)?
11. Is your screenplay, including your title page, properly formatted to industry standards? Is your formatting consistent?
12. Have you registered your final draft with the Writers Guild of America West?[1]

¶ *For more on screenplay writing and revision, see my book "Organic Screenwriting: Writing for Film, Naturally."*

---

[1] https://www.wgawregistry.org

14. Next Steps

Now this is not the end. It is not even the beginning of the end.
But it is, perhaps, the end of the beginning.
WINSTON CHURCHILL

Nobody can make you feel inferior without your consent.
ELEANOR ROOSEVELT

Now What?

There is a time to hold your work to yourself and a time to share it out into the world.

Once you have read your story so often that you've lost count and have moved through more drafts than you ever imagined possible, it's time to seek out other, more objective views. It's time to get feedback. (I prefer the word "feedback" to "critique." It sounds more supportive and less judgmental.)

- Start by having someone you trust and respect read your manuscript and give you *constructive* feedback. (See "The Seven Be's of Empowered Feedback" in the next chapter.)

- If you're part of a writers' group, consider sharing all or part of your final draft with fellow members. Alternatively, consider setting up a Heartful Art of Revision Feedback Circle. You'll find suggestions on how to do that in "Your Circle of Creative Support," later in this section.

- If you have written a screenplay or stage play, enlist actor friends to perform a read-through and ask for their professional feedback.

- Put out a call for beta readers. A beta reader is generally a non-professional who approaches your work as a *reader* rather than as a fellow writer to give you honest, unbiased feedback on any aspect of your work. Although beta readers are most often used for fiction, there's no reason you can't work with one for your nonfiction or script. See "Testing Your Work with Beta Readers," later in this section.

- Hire an editor. Why? I answer that question, also later in this section, in "Yes, Hire an Editor."

The Seven Be's of Empowered Feedback

Feedback *(noun)*: sympathetic vibration...
ROGET'S INTERNATIONAL THESAURUS

Feedback can be helpful or disruptive. It can foster your creative process or cripple it. It can match *Roget's* "sympathetic vibration" synonym or the screeching distortion of a malfunctioning sound system.

How do you ensure that others' views and comments support your writing project, not distort it? By following these Seven Be's of Empowered Feedback when you share your work — with anyone, including your best friend, your life partner, a colleague or members of your writers' group.

1. BE SELECTIVE

Seek out only those people who will support you and your work. Never assume that those closest to you will fall into that category. Often, without intending to hurt you, they are the most critical and least helpful.

When someone asks to read all or part of your story, always use your discernment and give yourself permission to say no when appropriate. Just because your best friends are writers (or, if you have written a screenplay, actors or directors) doesn't make them the best people from whom to seek feedback.

The same applies to writers' groups and critique groups. Get a sense of the group before joining, and once you are attending, note the type of feedback offered by its members before agreeing to share your work. The only reason to offer feedback is to support the writer and his or her work. Regardless of claims to the contrary, not all groups function in a manner that supports that philosophy.

¶ *Set up your own writers' group with the tips in "Your Circle of Creative Support," next chapter.*

2. Be Open

Don't be overprotective and suffocating. Don't let fear hold you back from sharing your work and your vision. Be open to others' perceptions and comments. At the same time, exercise discernment in determining which of those perceptions and comments are relevant and which can be dismissed at this moment in your work's development and yours.

3. Be Aware

To everything there is a season. At different stages in your work and in your creative process, you will be ready to hear different things. Respect where you are and seek only the type and depth of feedback you are prepared to receive, integrate and apply. Recognize when you are at your most raw and respect that too. As always, discernment is key.

4. Be Clear

Be clear within yourself about the type of feedback that is important to you at this stage of your revision journey. For example:

- Do you want to know what emotions your work elicits? Whether your reader found one of your scenes or the whole draft funny? Moving? Riveting? Suspenseful? Romantic? Sensual? Enlightening? Inspiring? Instructive?

- Do you want to know whether the reader identified with your protagonist? Whether your characters are original and credible? Whether your dialogue is natural or appropriate? Whether your sex scenes or scenes of violence are too graphic? Not graphic enough?

- Do you want to know whether the reader found your descriptions and imagery evocative?

- Do you want to know whether the reader found your arguments persuasive or convincing? Your ideas compelling? Your examples helpful? Your illustrations relevant? Your instructions clear?

- Are you looking for detailed line-by-line input? Suggestions about spelling, punctuation, grammar and other nitpicky details? Or are you interested only in general comments?

Only you can determine what will support your creative process at this time and what might damage it, so…

5. Be Explicit

Once you have determined the type and depth of feedback that is appropriate for you and your draft right now, ask for it — clearly, directly and with neither apology nor equivocation. Your reader cannot know how best to support you unless you make your needs clear.

Don't be shy or embarrassed to make those needs known. If you are vague, hesitant or unclear, you open yourself to comments you may not be ready to hear, comments that could feel hurtful or damaging, even if they are not intended to be so.

6. Be Strong

Know what you want and don't be afraid to speak up — lovingly, compassionately and, again, without apology — when you are not getting it, or when you are getting something you didn't ask for. This is your work and your creative process. You have every right to seek out what will help and support you as you travel the road to submission and/or publication/production. In this, you are not only training yourself to determine what will assist you, you are training your friends, family and fellow writers to provide feedback in supportive ways and to seek it for themselves in empowered ways.

7. Be Discerning

Deep inside, you know your work's strengths and weaknesses. Tap into that intuitive inner knowingness and rely on it to discern which comments it is wisest to ignore and which support you and serve your story.

Negative comments, whether intentionally cruel or not, have no power to harm you unless you abdicate your power and allow yourself to be hurt. (See also "Criticism Is Inevitable," later in this section.)

Seeking Feedback? Ask Yourself These Questions...

- How can I be clearer within myself about the feedback I require right now? How can I be clearer with others about the feedback I am seeking?
- How can I be more discerning about where and to whom I turn for feedback?
- How can I be more respectful of my story's needs and my own when seeking feedback?
- How can I be more discriminating in determining which feedback to take to heart and which to dismiss?

Offering Feedback? Ask Yourself These Questions...

- How can I listen more fully to the nature of the feedback that has been requested of me?
- How can I be clearer and more specific in the feedback I offer?
- How can I be more respectful of the work and its creator, offering feedback that doesn't show how clever I am but instead serves the needs and growth of the writer and his or her work?

Your circle of creative Support

Can't find a writers' group that offers supportive feedback? Consider setting up your own — a Heartful Art of Revision Feedback Circle. In coming together with other writers, you have an opportunity to take all you have experienced and read in these pages and multiply it manyfold.

These days, there's no need to be in the same city or on the same continent to form a feedback circle. Countless free and paid meeting and teleconference services make it possible for you to interact with fellow writers nearly anywhere in the world. All it takes is a computer or appropriate mobile device, a webcam, a high-speed internet link, some basic tech knowhow and a rudimentary grasp of global time zones.

However you format your Heartful Art of Revision Feedback Circle, consider including the following eight elements, all geared toward keeping the experience a supportive and productive one for all:

1. Check-In

Set aside time at the start of every get-together for all members to share writing, revision, feedback and/or submission experiences since the previous meeting.

2. Commitment

Have all members commit to reading all submitted material in time to offer relevant feedback.

3. Feedback

Decide whether your feedback circle will offer instant feedback on work read at each meeting, whether feedback will be limited to material circulated before the meeting or a combination of the two. Consider limiting each member's speaking time to ensure that everyone present gets a say. Have all members subscribe to "The Seven Be's of Empowered Feedback," including the "Offering Feedback?" questions at the end of the chapter.

4. Rotation

Take turns moderating and hosting the circle.

5. Frequency

Agree to meet regularly, at least monthly.

6. Numbers

Keep the size of your group small enough so that everyone has an opportunity to give and receive feedback — if not at every meeting, then at every second or third meeting.

7. Atmosphere

For in-person get-togethers, create a space and ambiance that is conducive to creativity and support, one that is quiet and where you and your fellow members won't be disturbed. Consider playing meditative music as people arrive to set the mood. People bond well over food, so many groups incorporate regular or occasional potlucks into their get-togethers.

If you are meeting via videoconference, urge all members to stay focused on your virtual circle by quitting all unnecessary applications and by muting all sounds and devices unrelated to the group experience.

8. Support

Your group exists for mutual support. Respect each other...and have fun!

Testing Your Work with Beta Readers

Just as beta testers review software for malfunctions that developers might have missed, beta readers report back on glitches that writers might have missed during the revision process. In both cases, of course, the testing is done *before* public release.

Beta readers are, most often, nonprofessionals who can offer you an ordinary reader's perspective. But they can also be fellow writers. Here, as with everything else on your creative journey, there are no rules. For example, you can work with one beta reader or, for a mix of opinions, several. And you can choose readers who are familiar with your topic or genre or those who are new to it; each has advantages and disadvantages. Or you can do both.

Regardless of who and how many you choose, incorporate these three guidelines:

1. Review "The Seven Be's of Empowered Feedback" before selecting your readers and be judicious about your choices. You want honest feedback that will improve the final work, not smart-ass comments that show nothing but how clever your readers think they are. Let your intuition help you choose.

2. Ask your readers some of the same questions you asked yourself in your "almost-final" read-through, as well as any from any other chapter in "Working with Your Drafts." Are there chapters, scenes, characters, arguments, illustrations or examples you're unsure of or insecure about? This is an ideal opportunity to get those concerns addressed. Be open, too, to unsolicited feedback. Beta readers are stand-ins for your ultimate readers, so why use these "test readers" if you're not prepared to hear what they have to say?

3. Be discerning about any feedback you receive. This is another opportunity to reread your vision statement and reconnect with your vision before accepting or rejecting any suggestions or criticisms.

Yes, Hire an Editor

You have run your writing project through multiple drafts and revisions, heeding the recommendations in earlier sections. You have followed Section 12's suggestion that you read your work as a "regular" reader might. Perhaps you have made changes to your script or manuscript based on the feedback of beta readers and fellow writers. And through it all, you have remained true to your vision. Why hire an editor?

When you have spent months or years immersed in a writing project you're passionate about, it becomes nearly impossible to view it impartially.

At your work's most basic level, there are typos, skipped/repeated words and confusing punctuation you will have missed, thanks to your brain's built-in autocorrect mechanism. For all your best efforts, that inner autocorrect will have tricked your eyes into seeing things that weren't there simply because they should have been or that were there when they were absent.

As well, your intimate knowledge of your story or subject material means there will inevitably be problems with your script or manuscript that you will not notice. There will also be some that your beta readers will not catch.

Even should your book be picked up by a traditional publisher, chances are your manuscript won't get the kind of in-depth edit for which publishers were once renowned. On the other hand, if it isn't well-edited, no publisher or agent will take it on.

And if you plan to publish it yourself, don't fortify the bad rap indie/self-published books once had, largely because they weren't properly edited.

It's no different with a stage play or screenplay. You want to make sure that what you submit has its best chance at being picked up and produced.

That's where the professional, objective eye of an editor or script/manuscript consultant comes in.

The three most common types of editing are:

1. Developmental / Substantive / Content / Consulting Editing

An in-depth look at your work that includes attention to elements like organization, structure, flow, logic, thesis/argument, plotting/storyline and characterization. It also looks at how these components function within individual chapters or scenes and within the work as a whole. While it might pick up copyediting and proofreading issues, that's not its primary objective. This is the sort of editing/consulting I do on book manuscripts and film scripts as an extension of my coaching/mentoring services.

2. Copyediting

Focuses on spelling, grammar, punctuation, style and usage.

3. Proofreading

Checks for typographical and related errors. Generally, this is the final edit before submission or publication.

Hiring an editor is a leap of faith. No editor, regardless of her credentials or his testimonials, can guarantee publication, production, glowing reviews or measurable success. However, hiring the *right* editor can guarantee that the work you put out into the world will be the best possible expression of your vision.

How do you find the right editor? There is no simple formula. Every editor is unique and all writers and writing projects have their individual needs.

Get referrals from fellow writers or from colleagues in publishing or, in the case of a screenplay, colleagues in the film industry. Or look to writing groups and professional associations for recommendations.

Talk to potential editors and share not only the nuts and bolts of your project but your vision for your work. You will be entering into what promises to be a close, ongoing relationship, especially when it comes to substantive editing, so do more than discuss credentials and fees. Use your intuitive and visionary senses to determine whether this could be a good match — for both you and your project. Reread your vision statement before any interview and again before making a final decision.

As with feedback from beta readers and others, you are not required to implement your editor's recommendations. Use your discernment to determine which best support your project and best align with your vision for it.

For example, the copy editor I hired for the first edition of *The Voice of the Muse* expressed concern about my dozen-plus references to "God" and urged me to delete them all. I weighed her arguments but decided that my use of the word, in a spiritual not religious context, was in perfect alignment with my vision for the book. The references stayed.

Finally, here's when *not* to hire an editor:

- after your first draft
- after your second draft
- when you have not yet done everything possible *on your own* to edit your script or manuscript and make it the most polished piece of work you can.

Criticism Is Inevitable

On January 1, 1962, Decca executives in London auditioned a little-known band for a grueling two hours and fifteen songs. After a nail-biting two-week wait, the band finally heard back from Decca's Dick Rowe: "Not to mince words, Mr. Epstein," Rowe wrote, "but we don't like your boys' sound." The manager was Brian Epstein; the group, The Beatles.

The Beatles, of course, proved Decca wrong, becoming one of the most successful bands of all time. As of 2014, the group had sold more than two billion singles.

Criticism and rejection are inevitable, and you can't count on Beatles-level success to soften the blow. When someone maligns your work, here are seven ways to help you get through and past the pain:

1. Cry, Curse, Scream

Don't bottle up your feelings. And don't get self-destructive. Feel what you feel. All of it. Cry. Curse. Yell. Scream. Throw things. Throw up. Then get past the criticism and move on.

2. Write Your Feelings

Powerful emotions birth powerful writing. Channel all the ways you're feeling into one of your characters — if not as part of this piece of work, then as part of another. You have no available story or character or aren't ready to create one? Journal your disappointment, rage and anguish.

3. Take Writer's Revenge

Write a scene where you subject whoever criticized you to something unspeakably hideous, hurtful and horrific. It's the writer's equivalent of sticking pins into a voodoo doll. Unless you write horror, this scene will likely never find its way into one of your stories, but you will have more fun writing it than you ever ought to admit.

4. Look for the Silver Lining

It sounds clichéd but it's true: Every experience, however emotionally debilitating, contains within it the seeds of something positive. You may not be able to see the redemptive value of this criticism today, and that's fine. But once the pain has subsided, be open to a flash of insight that will reveal the silver lining surrounding your storm cloud of rejection.

5. Look for the Spark of Truth

If someone has taken the time to offer feedback, pay attention to all the comments, including the harsh ones, and discern whether they highlight real weaknesses it would serve you to address in a new draft.

6. Keep Writing

A few years ago, *The MoonQuest* received a review so searing that I was surprised the reader gave it two stars, not one. For all I teach about how to handle rejection, the criticism cut deep and made it difficult for me to continue with the book I was then working on. Yet all we can do in the face of others' judgment and our own is to write on. That's what I did.

Don't let one rebuke or rejection — or one hundred or one thousand — stop you. Keep writing and keep seeking ways to become a better writer.

7. Believe in Yourself

Getting feedback can be an important part of the revision process as well as an important step on your creative journey. Seek feedback as a way to improve your work not to feel better about yourself as a writer. Seeking outside validation for your creation is an expression of lack of trust — in yourself and in your story. Believe in yourself!

Criticized or Rejected? Ask Yourself These Questions...

- Can I refuse to let criticism or rejection stop me from moving forward with this or any of my writing projects?
- If I am unable to get an agent, a publishing deal or a screenplay option, can I trust that there may be other reasons why I was called to write this? Can I be okay with that?

15. Finishing Up

The first draft reveals the art; revision reveals the artist.
MICHAEL LEE

"When I make a word do a lot of work like that,"
said Humpty Dumpty, "I always pay it extra."
LEWIS CARROLL

As Many as It Takes

One of the questions I'm asked most often by new writers is how many drafts it will take before their story is finished and ready for the world. The answer, as I noted in "Why Edit," is "as many as it takes."

I don't remember how many drafts *The MoonQuest* went through before it was published. What I do remember was that there were a lot — off and on over thirteen years.

I completed at least two "final" drafts during that time. After the first, convinced I was finished with *The MoonQuest*, I began work on its sequel, *The StarQuest*. A few years later, that first *MoonQuest* final draft would become the basis for my film adaptation of the book. That screenplay led to a new final draft of the novel.

That's because rewriting *The MoonQuest* as a movie forced me to view the story from a fresh perspective — through a different lens, if you will — and that fresh perspective sparked changes worthwhile enough to retrofit back into the novel. The script was optioned, which was terrific. More important for our purposes, though, the exercise proved to be a powerful revision tool. (I talk more about adapting your novel for the screen in my book *Organic Screenwriting: Writing for Film, Naturally*.)

Thirteen years may seem like a long time to get from conception to publication. It sure felt that way. As it turned out, it took *The StarQuest* fifteen. So I was understandably relieved (and astounded) when *The Way of the Fool* took only ten *weeks*. Most of my books have fallen somewhere in between.

Here, too, there are neither rules nor standards. In a survey a few years back, writers were asked, "How long has your book or writing project been in progress?" Nearly half, 45.2 percent, answered, "longer than I care to think about or admit." The next-largest group, 19 percent, said their writing project had been in progress for one to five years.

For most of us, the journey from conception to completion probably takes longer than we care to think about or admit, whoever we are and whatever that translates into in months or years. It's also likely to involve more drafts than most of us would prefer.

Three drafts or thirty? Ten weeks or fifteen years? How many is "as many as it takes"? Turn the page to find out.

"How Do I Know When I'm Finished?"

After "how many drafts does it take," the second most frequently asked question I get, and not only from new writers, is "how do I know when I'm finished?"

Again, there is no rule or universal standard. Every writing project is different. The only answer I can offer is this: You're finished when, given your skill at this stage of your craft, you have done your best to polish, enrich and enliven your work so it aligns with your vision, while recognizing that no final draft is ever perfect.

When you reach that point, trusting your discernment and intuition to guide you, let it go. Celebrate your achievement. Get your work out into the world by submitting it to agents or publishers or by publishing/producing it yourself. Then create a new work and do your best on that one as well.

After all, you're a writer. A writer writes.

16. Final Thoughts

If I waited for perfection I would never write a word.
MARGARET ATWOOD

It always seems impossible until it's done.
NELSON MANDELA

Trust Your Vision, Trust Your Story

It's March 1995, a chilly spring morning in rural Nova Scotia. With notepad on my lap, pen in hand and a fire crackling in the Kemac stove, I begin the day's work on *The MoonQuest*, grateful that this first draft is nearly finished. To my surprise, what emerges onto the page is not my usual third-person narrative. Instead, I find myself writing in the first person as Toshar, the story's main character.

It doesn't take me long to realize that Toshar's voice is the story's voice and that for my next draft, I will have to rewrite *The MoonQuest* from scratch, from his perspective. To do it, I know I will have to delete many scenes, add new ones and subject those that survive to wholesale revision.

My old editor-self would have approached the task as an exercise in left-brain mechanics. My new, intuitive inner editor recognizes the need for a more holistic approach.

Instead of shoehorning *The MoonQuest* into the first-person, I choose to treat the story as a sentient entity and let it tell me what is necessary and what is expendable. Instead of trying to figure out which scenes to retain and which to cut, I choose to free the story to find its own retelling through me.

If my experience in writing my first *MoonQuest* draft on the Muse Stream has helped me trust in the wisdom of the story, I now allow myself to trust it yet more deeply in revising it. The result? My second draft surges out of me with an ease and speed I neither expected nor could have imagined.

How did I do it?

- by listening for the voice of the story and its characters
- by listening *to* the voice of the story and its characters
- by trusting the story's innate wisdom and surrendering to it, unconditionally

In other words, by getting out of my own way, respecting my vision, following my intuition and practicing discernment.

The result? *The MoonQuest* went on to win multiple awards and earn dozens of enthusiastic reviews. I share that not to brag but to demonstrate that whole-brain editing works. And if it works for me, it can work for you...whatever you are working on.

In "12½ Secrets to Whole-Brain Editing" (Section 6), I insisted that there are no rules for heartful revision. Perhaps, though, there's one: Do whatever it takes to make your writing clearer, to let your vision shine through on the page and to honor the work that chose you to transform its infinite energy into words.

You owe it to your work. You owe to yourself.

Now, get to work and let your writing be the masterpiece it deserves to be.

You Are a Writer

A Guided Meditation

I include this meditation in all my books for writers because it is too easy, as creative artists working largely in isolation, to diminish ourselves and our output and to forget that we are powerful and empowered creators.

Listen to this meditation when you feel doubt...when you feel less-than... when you don't believe you will ever be able to finish this project...when you question whether you are a writer.

In those moments, let the words and spirit of this meditation remind you that you are a writer — of power, passion, strength and courage. For writing is an act of courage...of immeasurable courage!

Allow 5 minutes for this meditative experience.

My professional recording of this meditation is available for download or streaming as part "The Voice of the Muse Companion: Guided Meditations for Writers." See "Guided Meditations" in Section 1 to find out how to access the recording, as well as for tips on how best to use this book's meditations.

Close your eyes and take a few deep breaths as you relax and listen...

You are a writer. You are a writer of power, passion, strength and, yes, courage. For writing is an act of courage. Acknowledge that courage, the courage that got you to this point...having written. Having written today, if you have. Having written just now, if you have.

You are a writer. Breathe in to that. Breathe in to the release you felt as the pen flowed across the page, as letters formed into words, words stretched into sentences and sentences began to fill your pages.

Breathe in to the freedom, the vibrancy, the love. Breathe in to the knowledge and knowingness that you can do it again. And again. And again. And again.

You are a writer. What you write is powerful. What you write is vibrant. What you write, whatever you believe in this moment, is luminous.

Trust that to the best of your ability, in this moment. Acknowledge the writer you are, in this moment. Breathe in to that.

Breathe out judgment. Breathe out fear. Breathe out not-good-enoughs. Breathe out comparisons. What others have written does not matter. What you have written is all that matters now, in this moment. It is perfect...in this moment. Know that. Trust that. Breathe in to that.

If you don't feel ready to read what you have written from that place of trust, discernment and compassion, set it aside. Set it aside for a time — until you arrive at a place of more clarity, more objectivity, more self-love.

Don't avoid reading it, but nor need you rush into it. Either way, for now know that you are a writer. A writer writes. That's what you have done. You have written.

You are a *writer.*

You *are* a writer.

You are a writer.

You have heard the words. Now speak them with me...

I am a *writer.*

I *am* a writer.

I am a writer.

Speak them again and again and again, knowing them to be true.
Speak them again, feeling the truth in them.
Speak them again, for they are true.

Share Your Vision

What vision statement did you come up with for your story or for yourself as the writer you are? I'd love to hear it. More than that, I'd love to hear how your vision statement has assisted you with the writing project that brought you to this book or with any writing project. And if your vision has in some way clarified or altered your approach to your art and craft, I'd love to hear about that as well.

To that end I have created a dedicated private page on my website — www.markdavidgerson.com/yourstories — and I invite you to share your experiences and vision statements there. What you post will not be shared publicly unless you give me explicit permission to do so, with or without your name. If you are open to having me post all or part of your contribution — in my newsletter and/or on social media — also include your work's title and a purchase link, if you have one.

While I can't promise to respond to or post every submission, I will read them all and get back to you wherever possible. I look forward with great anticipation to hearing from you. Meantime, good luck...and write on!

About the Author

Mark David Gerson is the founder of The Mark David Gerson School of Writing, as well as a screenwriter and the award-winning author of more than twenty books. His nonfiction includes classic titles for writers, inspiring personal growth books and compelling memoirs. As a novelist he is best known for *The Legend of Q'ntana* fantasy series, coming soon to movie theaters, and *The Sara Stories*, set largely in his native Canada.

When not writing, Mark David coaches an international roster of both first-time and seasoned writers to help them get their stories onto the page and into the world with ease.

Visit Mark David's website at www.markdavidgerson.com, and follow him on Facebook at www.facebook.com/markdavidgerson.

More Writing Inspiration!

www.ingramcontent.com/pod-product-compliance
Lightning Source LLC
Chambersburg PA
CBHW030320100526
44592CB00010B/505